SUCCESS

BRIDGING THE GAP BETWEEN WHERE
YOU ARE NOW AND WHERE YOU WANT TO BE
TO ACHIEVE MASSIVE SUCCESS

Rachel M. Stewart

Printed in the United States of America
First Printing, 2019
ISBN 978-1-7336925-0-2

www.unqualifiedtools.com

DEDICATION

To my family.

Kent, thank you for your love, support, and sacrifice as I have spent the last decade climbing my Everest. More than once, you have scaled those treacherous cliffs to bring me oxygen and keep me moving through the storms. I adore you and couldn't do any of this without you.

Beautiful, talented, and precious children, thank you for believing in me. I hope you always see the possibilities, the hope, and the adventure in reaching for your dreams.

Contents

Acknowledgements..i

CHAPTER 1 UNQUALIFIED 1
Exercises For Application 11

CHAPTER 2 MINDSET MATTERS.......................................15
Exercises To Change Your Mindset.................................... 27

CHAPTER 3 BELIEF IN ACTION 31
Exercises To Change Belief 39

CHAPTER 4 FAKE IT 'TIL YOU MAKE IT 45
Exercises To Realize Your Future Self................................. 57

CHAPTER 5 VISION 61
Exercises To Expand Your Vision..77

CHAPTER 6 GRIT 81
Exercises To Grow Grit 93

CHAPTER 7 FEAR.. 97
Exercises To Manage Fear 111

CHAPTER 8 FAILURE... 115
Exercises For Using Failure To Fuel Success.................... 131

CHAPTER 9 HUNGRY FOR GROWTH..............................135
Exercises For Growth 149

CHAPTER 10 PERSISTENCE...155
Exercises In Persistence.. 171

CHAPTER 11 VULNERABILITY...175
Exercises In Vulnerability...191

CHAPTER 12 SHOWING UP..197
Exercises For Showing Up 215

CHAPTER 13 RIPPLE EFFECT 221
Exercises To Create The Ripple Effect 237

CHAPTER 14 UNQUALIFIED AND SUCCESSFUL.................................... 239
Exercises To Be An Unqualified Success 249

About The Author..251

ACKNOWLEDGEMENTS

This book would not be in your hands without the help and love of so many.

First, Russ Palmer who opened that first door for me and generously continues to provide opportunities for my growth and possibility. His ripple effect on my life truly cannot be measured. Along with Russ, my extraordinary teams at Titan and Xcelerate have patiently supported me as I practiced the principles of unqualified success with them. I will always be grateful for the chance to lead such capable and driven people.

Next, my mentor and friend, John Chatwin, who believes in me unequivocally—no matter the goal and no matter my lack of qualification. I am equally grateful to my other coaches and mentors, Phil Rosebrook, Howard Shore, and Les Cunningham, who always challenge me to push my own boundaries and reach for something higher.

I am lucky to work with incredible industry colleagues, including Bill Weber, Nathan Link, Sami Erhart, Heather Biggs, and Greg Anapol, whose proofreading, feedback, and insight were instrumental in the creation of this book as well as so many other aspects of my career. Their opinions have been extremely valuable, honest, and perceptive.

I am immeasurably grateful to the achievers I have written about in this book who have shown us all what is possible and whose powerful stories make us all better. Especially Magno Santos, whose bravery, faith, and tenacity will always inspire me.

Everything began for me at home, and anything I have accomplished or achieved I owe to the stalwart example of my parents who never give up, never yield to fear, and never stop believing—especially in me. I am grateful for their invaluable help with this project and the unending love and cheerleading they always provide in my life. Also, my sister, April Price, who from the first text, "I think I'm going to write a book," championed my idea and put her own goals on the back burner to help me reach my own.

Madeleine L'Engle once wrote: "If we are qualified, we tend to think that we have done the job ourselves. If we are forced to accept our evident lack of qualification, then there's no danger that we will confuse God's work with our own, or God's glory with our own." It's nice to know I have never been in this kind of danger. Christ, who is whole, makes up all my deficiencies and covers for all my shortcomings. It is only by His mercy and grace that I can do anything at all.

CHAPTER 1

UNQUALIFIED

"Whatever I did, there was always someone around who was better qualified. They just didn't bother to do it."

-James A. Michener

I am unqualified to write this book.

Before you go running back to Amazon to demand a refund, please note that I did give you ample warning. The title is a large caution label plastered right across the front, clearly letting you know the state of things: I am unqualified.

And yet you purchased it anyway. Why? We both know it isn't because you have time to waste. The amount of pressure you are under and the number of plates you are trying to spin is staggering. Your time is valuable. There is always work to be done. People are depending on you.

So unless you are my editor or a very good friend, you bought this book and invested your time because in some aspect of your life you feel unqualified too.

Unqualified for the job you want? Check.

Unqualified for the job you have? Check.

Unqualified to be a parent? Check.

Unqualified to be the right leader to meet the issues your business faces every day? Check.

Unqualified to change and uplevel your life? Check.

Unqualified to get the big wins? Check.

Unqualified to grow and adapt at the pace that is required in today's ever-changing world? Check.

Unqualified to create a culture that engages your employees, keeps them motivated, and helps them progress? Check.

Unqualified to hit the lofty goals ahead of you and then raise the bar and hit them again? Check.

Unqualified to live the life you've always wanted? Check.

Unqualified to see your dreams become a reality? Check. Check. Check.

The truth is that all of us are unqualified. No, really! You are not alone. If you don't feel unqualified in some major aspects of your life, then you are either living way below your potential in a way that doesn't require you to stretch and grow, or you have so much innate confidence and bold ego that there is clearly no need to continue reading.

For the rest of us, this book is about learning to bridge the gap between where you are now and where you want to be. It is about understanding how your feelings of inadequacy and fear and insufficiency are holding you back *unnecessarily*. Unqualified is only a state of mind. It is not an accurate reflection of your actual abilities nor your capacity to succeed. For each of us, both of these factors are categorically unlimited. It is only the universal feeling of being unqualified that is holding us back.

I was recently at a conference for an organization made up of successful entrepreneurs. In order to even apply to be a part of the group, you have to meet certain thresholds in revenue and growth, meaning that everyone in the organization is, by any standards, highly qualified.

While I was at the conference, I shared the fact that I felt like I had just "fallen off the turnip truck" and it wasn't even a very nice turnip truck. I felt out of my depth around so many high achievers. After my comment, a member of the prestigious group shared a story.

He said that he had been invited to speak at the national conference for this same organization and give a 10-minute talk. The 10-minute talks are supposed to be $250,000 ideas—ways to help people grow their businesses by $250,000 in ten minutes. My highly-qualified colleague had been invited to speak because of his ability and reputation. He gave the talk which was very well-received and returned to his seat.

Following his talk was a 30-minute presentation given by someone else on consumer behavior, which happens to be my colleague's area of expertise. My colleague said the presentation that followed his was so good that he went into the lobby afterwards and cried. He was overwhelmed by his own inadequacy and lack. He was overcome by what he felt was "his obvious inability to offer something valuable to the other participants." In that moment, he felt wholly unqualified in every way.

The point is, he said, no matter where you are in your career or in the path of your life, you will always *feel* unqualified. *This does not mean you are unqualified.* The aim of this book is to help you gain awareness of this important differentiation and then manage any feelings of insufficiency in order to do your work in the world.

Michelle D. Craig recently said, "Each of us, if we are honest, feels a gap between where and who we are, and where and who we want to become. We yearn for greater personal capacity. These feelings create an urgency to act."

It is likely this urgency to act and find greater personal capacity that has prompted you to read this book. You want more—more from yourself, more from your life, more from your future. I know from experience, it's possible to get it.

MY STORY

My own story started 10 years ago when I was hired as a completely unqualified bookkeeper and office manager. Technically, I had never managed anyone's books. I had never run an office. My job was with a restoration company and I was completely unfamiliar with the industry. On top of all that, I had been out of the working world for a good five years as I had been home raising my little family. Written out like that, it kind of makes you wonder why they hired me, right?

The circumstances around my return to work were in part because of the Great Recession that hit the country at the end of 2008. My husband lost his job and made the decision to become an independent insurance broker and build his own agency. My youngest child was eight months old and I had two others at home, ages three and five. We, like so many others, were upside-down on our house, which we had purchased at the height of the housing market boom two years earlier. Seemingly overnight, my husband had lost his job and our home had lost half of its value. To say that we were living with a good deal of fear and uncertainty is putting it mildly.

The way I was hired can be described in no other way than divine intervention. I had not put out a resumé, I had not even made the conscious decision to go back to work despite our situation. The most I had done was have worry-filled conversations with my husband, lying in our bed at night, as we tried to determine the best course of action for our future.

Part of the problem, I thought, was that technically speaking, I really wasn't qualified to do much. I hadn't finished my degree in political science. At the time, I was dabbling on the side, doing self-taught graphic design work and book layout, but the majority of my time and focus was spent doing puppet shows, reading bedtime stories, washing dirty faces and hands, and keeping tiny humans alive.

Years before, my husband, Kent, had met Russ Palmer in the accounting program at Arizona State University. Russ had a little carpet cleaning van that he used to pay his way through school. Somewhere in the middle of those jobs, he got exposed to water losses and flood dryouts and instantly fell in love with the science and methodology behind restoration. He learned everything he could about it and started a small restoration company.

Russ and Kent stayed in touch occasionally after they left school, but weren't close friends. I had only briefly met Russ once. One day in November of 2008, Russ reached out to Kent. He was looking for a recommendation for an office manager/bookkeeper for his restoration company. Kent said, "Well for my money, I'd hire my wife."

On my first day of work, I showed up at the small, dated, farmhouse which was Titan Restoration's existing office space. The two other full-time workers and I worked on folding tables set up in the kitchen because it was the best-lit room in the house. Paper files cluttered the floors and available counter spaces. Even to my inexperienced eye, the accounting books were a mess.

I soon came to realize that the "accounts department" was really only a "document generation station"—invoices were created and sent to customers, but actually receiving money or payments in return was hit or miss. The receivables were not actually reliably being received. It was nearly impossible to determine who really owed us money, our annual revenue amounts, the health of our balance sheet, or what our cash status really was. The last time the bank account had been reconciled was right before never. Basically, I had just walked into my dream job.

When I was growing up, one of my favorite pastimes was jigsaw puzzles. Over holiday breaks, my family would break out a new puzzle and go to work creating order and beauty from chaos. As I got older, I would try to make it even more challenging by mixing up several puzzles in one box and then putting them together. The more challenging the better. That's exactly what the next eight months felt like as I tried to decipher how all the pieces of the business fit together and locate the missing pieces tucked away in the corners of the farmhouse and in giant stacks of old paperwork.

There was a lot I didn't know. (Surprising, I know, especially given my level of qualification.) I started with understanding a P&L and a balance sheet and devouring everything I could google, read, or listen to about the topic. Simultaneously, I learned everything I could about the restoration industry. I organized, strategized, documented, planned, systematized, standardized, revamped, and reconciled. I progressed, succeeded, failed, floundered, rallied, triumphed, and continued. Above all, I worked, and worked, and worked some more. There were days that were frustrating and demoralizing, and there were days that were incredibly satisfying and fulfilling.

Overall the experience was exhilarating because, at its core, I could see I worked for a really phenomenal company. I could see the DNA of something great—a company that, although it didn't have efficient processes or an organized back office, really knew restoration. Russ Palmer was the best in the industry when it came to structural drying. The end-user experience was great and he had created fantastic relationships along the way. The ethics and integrity of the company were high and the small team of people we had were committed and passionate. Titan had all the raw materials to be remarkable and I could see the reality of a future great company even in the early days.

When I was finally able to wrangle order out of QuickBooks and was able to get true financial statements, it was a great day. We were then doing $1.3M in annual revenue. Russ laid out his five-year goal: Get the company to $5M and sell. We went to work to make that happen. Two years later we had hit that milestone and Russ wanted out of the day-to-day operations of the company.

He began talks with another local restoration company and there were very serious discussions about a merger. In fact, things were so far down the path to merge, that Titan had actually moved into the building of the other company. But it wasn't a good move for Russ. He would go from being a sole owner to being one of six other owners in a company that was not nearly as profitable. I kept asking him to consider bringing in an outside, highly-experienced General Manager or CEO to run daily operations, and he could have as much or as little involvement as he wanted. We could put an ad out, talk to our network, hire a headhunter, and find the best-qualified person. The day that papers for the merger were to be signed, Russ backed out of the deal.

A week later, Russ and our hired consultant offered me the General Manager position. I was shocked, fearful, excited, hungry, and ecstatic. I told both of them that I had no experience, no qualification, no references—nothing but a commitment to figure it out, learn everything I could, incredible determination and grit to drive the company vision, and the belief that Titan was the best company in the world.

It hasn't always been butterflies and rainbows. Along the way, I have had some really low days when I wondered if I could indeed make the vision a reality. I saw the gap between where I was and where I wanted to go, and the seeing was painful.

One memorable moment occurred in 2016. We had just hired Howard Shore, an experienced and very successful executive coach who specializes in accelerating the scalability and growth of companies. His track record and the pedigree of companies he had worked with was impressive. We were having our first quarterly retreat with our executive team. It did not go well. In fact, it ended with a significant amount of tears on my part, something that isn't a common occurrence in my personal life, let alone in a professional setting. I was humiliated, frustrated, and a little bit angry. Russ called me that night and asked if I thought we needed to hire a new coach. In a moment of clarity, I replied, "No. You may need to hire a new General Manager, but I think you have the right coach."

That statement couldn't have been more true. The last several years have been significant in my growth, both professionally and personally. I now consider Howard a dear friend and our relationship and trust has evolved to the point that we are now business partners on a software solution for restoration contractors. Howard is one of the most skilled and effective business coaches in the world. Being able to work with him personally is a rare privilege. There is a waiting list of companies that want to work with him and his firm. I look back on that moment when I could have protected my ego, worried about my positioning, operated from a place of fear, let my inadequacies and insufficiencies protect and hold me back, by telling Russ that Howard was the wrong fit for Titan and that we needed to find a different coach. That would have been a massive, growth-impeding, life-altering mistake for both the company and myself.

Titan ended the last quarter of 2018 with $22M in revenue, with record-breaking profits, high levels of excellence and customer service, a strong company culture, and impressive employee retention. Not only that but Titan has gained a position of respect in the industry, taking several leadership positions, and winning awards for business excellence. We have no plans to slow down; in fact, we are just starting to hit our stride.

This book isn't about ego. In fact, it's about the exact opposite. I have been highly unqualified for every position I have ever held. But I have come to learn that we all are. We are all unqualified today for the life we could have tomorrow.

That idea should not be disheartening. It should light you up. It should spark a fire in your heart. It means that the possibilities for achievement and growth are endless, and that your "qualification" has nothing to do with getting either one. There are horizons after horizons after horizons. And you are unqualified for every one of them until you get there and see the next one out there in the distance. Could there be anything more inspiring? Facing, managing, and partnering with our unqualification is the way we get there. Who's with me?

EXERCISES FOR APPLICATION

While we all have feelings of inadequacy that hold us back from realizing our potential, it is the goal of this book to help you manage those feelings and overcome them so that you can achieve any success you want.

In the upcoming chapters of the book, I will introduce a new principle that will help you conquer your "unqualified" feelings. I have included exercises at the end of each chapter to help you apply the things we have discussed.

These exercises are always optional, of course, but I believe that if you take the time and energy to do them and put your thoughts and intentions on paper, you will make enormous progress in managing the unqualified feelings that are holding you back. These practical application exercises will give you an awareness of your own mind and equip you with real tools to create the results you want in your life. Additional exercises and examples can be found on our website:
www.unqualifiedtools.com

On the website there is also a place for you to share your own experiences and get feedback as you apply the principles of *Unqualified Success* in your life. Your insights and personal application will help others on their own journeys, and I appreciate your participation in our community of unqualified achievers.

I invite you to go all in—to not just read and consume this information—but act and produce the real results you want in your life.

In 1994, Magno Santos was a young married man living in Sao Paolo, Brazil. He had a wife and a new daughter and he worked hard at two different jobs to provide for them. He worked nights at the Sao Paolo airport at a rental car counter, helping travelers get transportation when they landed in the city. At six in the morning, he would head home and sleep for a few hours before getting on his motorcycle and heading to his second job where he picked up checks for the banks. He had a route that he would drive during rush hour, stopping at 10 different banks along the way, putting all the collected checks from the day's transactions into a large backpack, and delivering them to the central bank in downtown Sao Paolo for processing.

"One night, I was at work at the airport and a gentleman asked me to help him fill out his boarding pass me and I saw that he was flying to the United States. I asked him, 'What are you going to do in the United States?' He told me, 'I'm gonna go there and work in a pizza place making pizza.'"

Magno asked him, "Do you speak English?" He didn't.

Magno asked him, "Do you read or write in English?" He didn't.

Then Magno asked him, "How much will they pay you to do that?" The man answered, "$1000 a month."

Magno thought the man was kidding. $1000 a month was a fortune!

Magno went home excited and told his wife about the man he had met. "He doesn't know how to read or write in Portuguese, let alone English. He can't speak any English. And he's still going to make more money than I do here, working two jobs and risking my life on the motorcycle. Can you imagine what I could do there? $1000 a month delivering pizza!"

That was the trigger.

This thought, that he could make $1000 a month delivering pizzas, caused Magno Santos to take action. That thought created a feeling of possibility and excitement. After that thought, nothing would ever be the same for him.

With this thought fueling him, Magno went into action. He sold everything he had. He sold their car, their furniture, the baby's crib, the house. Everything he could sell, he did, in order to buy the tickets to get to America. They boarded the plane with $200 left in their pockets and flew to Miami. When they landed, Magno quickly realized that he didn't even know enough English to order food. In America, Magno was even unqualified to buy a cheeseburger.

From there they flew to Salt Lake City to stay with Magno's sister. It was November 24, 1994, the day after Thanksgiving. There was snow on the ground, and Magno described it as "enchantingly beautiful." They had made it. The thought of what was possible had completely altered Magno's mindset. This seismic shift propelled Magno to action and resulted in a dramatic change in his circumstances, but it all began as an idea in his mind.

CHAPTER 2

MINDSET MATTERS

"The consummate truth of life is that we alter our destiny by altering our thoughts."

-Dr. Dennis Deaton

As we start our journey from feeling unqualified to becoming an unqualified success, one of the most important factors is your mindset. This is far more than just positive thinking. This is harnessing the tangible, literal power of your thoughts to create the life you want.

Feeling unqualified is not pleasant. It's uncomfortable and unnerving and reminds us that we are vulnerable. To avoid this, most of us who feel unqualified in any area of our lives look for a way to feel better. It is natural to assume that our feelings are giving us an accurate picture of reality: if we *feel* unqualified, perhaps we *are* unqualified.

When we see things in this way, it seems like the answer to feeling bad is to work hard at becoming "qualified." We think if we put in enough effort and take lots of action, then we will get the results we want and can finally stop feeling unqualified. And while it is true that hard work is a huge piece of the equation (I happen to have a very good chapter about it), it is not the starting point. Taking action is never the place to start. Instead, everything needs to begin in our minds. If you are approaching success without looking first at mindset, you are going to spend a lot of time working against yourself.

Let's take a closer look at how this works. Most people think the formula for feeling qualified is:

TAKE ACTION $\longrightarrow$ GET RESULTS $\longrightarrow$ FEEL GOOD

We have been taught this pattern throughout our whole lives. Accomplishing things is what makes us feel good, right? That's why most of us pursue goals in the first place—because of the way we think it will make us feel after we accomplish it.

SET GOALS & WORK HARD $\longrightarrow$ ACHIEVE GOAL $\longrightarrow$ FEEL QUALIFIED

The trouble with this model is that both the premise and the methodology are flawed. We can't feel better through achievement or by taking any amount of action because our feelings are only created by our thoughts. Working on our actions and behaviors without working on our mindset is one of the primary reasons we aren't getting the results we want in our lives.

BACK TO SCHOOL

I have a friend who wanted to feel qualified in her field as a family counselor. She earned her master's degree in marriage and family therapy, but still did not feel fully qualified to work as a therapist, so she went on and got her Ph.D. She was taking lots of action to feel ready and able to do her work as a counselor. Still feeling unsure that she had all the tools she might need after earning her doctorate, she decided to pursue an additional degree in positive psychology from the University of Pennsylvania. Surely then she would feel qualified to set up a practice and help families navigate their difficulties.

Even though she was taking lots of ACTION and was earning plenty of qualifying degrees as a RESULT, she still did not have the FEELING of being qualified.

$$\frac{ACTION}{go\ back\ to\ school} \rightarrow \frac{RESULT}{Earn\ multiple\ degrees} \neq \frac{FEELING}{qualified}$$

This is because our feelings *never* come from our results. Our feelings are only ever created by our thoughts. This is hard to recognize because achievement can indeed give us thoughts that make us feel good. We then associate feelings with results. But be careful to note that the results themselves are not creating the feelings—our thoughts *about* the results are. Feelings are only ever created by our thoughts.

This may just seem like semantics, but it is actually the critical differentiation we must make in order to start achieving real results in our lives.

My friend thought she would feel better after she had more education. But her results, no matter how impressive, could not change her deep-seated, underlying thought that she was not ready or prepared enough to be a counselor, and so she could never feel qualified, no matter how much action (schooling) she took or how many results (degrees) she got.

In order to have a different feeling we have to have a different mindset. No amount of action and no amount of achievement will ever be able to offset the thoughts you believe about yourself. Qualification, like so many other things, exists in our mind. As we see with my friend, there is no piece of paper, trophy, award, promotion, or pronouncement that can ever override the power of your own beliefs.

Let me illustrate with another example. About six years ago, a new mentoring program was created for women working in venture capital and private equity firms. Several high-level managing finance directors were approached about being part of the program. Many of them were excited to participate. However, all of those interested wanted to enroll in the "mentee side" of the program.

The program organizer reported to Pacific Standard Magazine[1] that though they had lots of interest in the program, none of the participants who registered to attend—regardless of their title—thought they "were experienced enough to be mentors," nor did they think they had anything of substance to offer someone else. One candidate, Katherine Anderson said, "It's sort of surprising to me that even when you get to the top, you still don't realize you've made it there."

The reason for this was not the women's actual qualifications. It was not their schooling or their resume or their years of experience. It was not about the projects or accounts they have managed or the size of the funds they supervised. It was only because of *how they thought* about their own qualifications and abilities.

In another example, the incoming students of the discriminating Harvard Business School are regularly surveyed at the beginning of their coursework, and asked: "How many of you in here feel that you are the one mistake that the admissions committee made?" When asked, two-thirds of these highly-qualified students raise their hands.

What we clearly learn from these and other examples is that *actual success* does not create the *feeling of success* or

---

[1] Friedman, Ann. "Not Qualified for Your Job? Wait, You Probably Are." Pacific Standard Magazine. Last modified October 22, 2013. Accessed February 25, 2019. https://psmag.com/economics/ qualified-job-wait-probably-imposter-syndrome-psychology-68700.

qualification. No matter the degree, the title, or the acceptance, the accomplishment didn't make any of these achievers feel better. They each still felt unqualified. This is because success and achievement of any kind is a result. And results never create feelings. This means that the model we are operating under—take action to get results to feel better—is flawed. This is where the importance of mindset comes into play.

BACK TO THE DRAWING BOARD

We must make a fundamental shift in understanding how to get the feelings we want. First, we must recognize, as we saw in the examples above, that results don't create feelings. Ever. If they did, the Harvard Business School students would feel qualified after being accepted. Yet, most of them don't. When the HBS students think, "The admissions committee made a mistake," they feel unqualified. No matter why the student was actually admitted, that thought is what creates their unqualified feeling.

Only our thoughts create feelings. When we think a thought, the brain releases certain chemicals in our body, giving us a feeling. This feeling makes us act or not act and we get a result. Understanding this truth can change everything for you because it allows you to access your ability to achieve *at the source*.

When we operate from an unqualified mindset, the brain produces chemicals that give us the feeling of fear or uncertainty or nervousness or anxiety or something similar. When we act from this feeling, we won't get the results we want.
Let's use the HBS students as an example:

THOUGHT	FEELING	ACTION	RESULT
The admissions committee made a mistake	Unqualified	Worry, ruminate; don't feel confident enough to fully invest; don't ask questions (because you don't want to look dumb)	Don't show up as the student you want to be; "prove" the admissions committee made a mistake

Isn't it interesting how when we feel unqualified it doesn't motivate us to be better? Those feelings just keep us from showing up as our best selves and we end up with less than desirable results.

Instead of running around trying to accomplish things so you can feel better, you need to feel better *first,* which will drive much more powerful action and give you better outcomes in your life. A positive mindset produces entirely different feelings—confidence, determination, certainty, courage—which ultimately create the results you want.

THOUGHT	FEELING	ACTION	RESULT
I belong here	Confidence	Work hard; ask questions; form study groups; give it all your best effort	Show up as your best self; "prove" you belong there

Really understanding the power of the right mindset allows you to question and examine your feeling of inadequacy for what they are: they are not helping you accomplish your goals and more importantly, they are created by your thoughts and not your resumé.

Let's talk about how to apply this in your life. First, remember that every emotion we experience is caused by a thought (and is not created in any other way). Second, remember that emotion is the fuel for any action or inaction we are taking in our lives. With these two principles in place, our formula for achievement looks like this:

THOUGHT $\longrightarrow$ FEELING $\longrightarrow$ ACTION $\longrightarrow$ RESULT

Our thoughts create our feelings which drive our actions which give us results.

As you look at this model a few things should stand out:

1. You need to have the feeling you want BEFORE you take action to achieve your desired result.
2. You will need to think the right thoughts in order TO CREATE those feelings.

Let's look at another example to demonstrate this.

Thomas is an emergency room director who would like to advance to VP of operations over the hospital. He's worried that he doesn't have enough experience for the job.

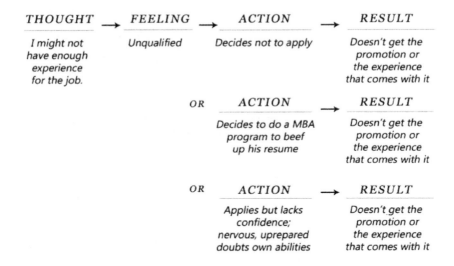

Do you see that no amount or type of action will change Thomas's feeling of being unqualified because his feeling is created by a thought? If Thomas has to wait to get a promotion in order to feel qualified, he might wait forever.

Likewise, it's also important to note that if Thomas holds on to his feeling of being unqualified, he will never get the result he wants, no matter what action he takes. Our results always prove our thoughts correct. Our brains love to be right. In fact, they want to be right even more than they want us to reach our goals. Note then, that every current result in your life is simply a result of a thought you are having.

The good news here is that the only thing Thomas has to do to get a different result is change his thought (or his mindset) in order to then change his feelings and drive a completely different action.

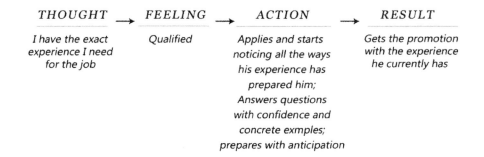

THOUGHT →	FEELING →	ACTION →	RESULT
I have the exact experience I need for the job	Qualified	Applies and starts noticing all the ways his experience has prepared him; Answers questions with confidence and concrete exmples; prepares with anticipation	Gets the promotion with the experience he currently has

But, you say, *how can he think that new thought if it isn't true?* Here's the magic: it is true if he believes it is. That is the only qualification. It turns out that the thought that he is qualified is just as true as his thought that he doesn't have enough experience. He can find evidence for both, depending on what he believes.

Our thoughts and our words have power. And the bottom line is that no one is qualified—not really. No matter how far we have come there is always a new step. We all have flaws and things to learn. But how we *think* about our capacity, our ability to grow and meet the challenges ahead, makes all the difference. The thought that is true is the one we choose to believe.

I don't want to overstate it, but this is the secret to the universe.

In traditional goal setting, we spend all our energy and focus on the action part of the equation. But even if you're taking tons of action towards your goal, if it is fueled by negative emotions it won't get you the results you want. Let's go back and look at my friend as an example:

THOUGHT →	FEELING →	ACTION →	RESULT
I might not know enough to be able to help people	Unqualified	Gets further education; applies for more programs	Gets more degrees but is still not helping people

If she wants to be able to feel confident enough to help people, she is going to have to change the thought/feeling part of the equation and stop working on the action/result side.

Hopefully, it is clear that all of your energy and effort needs to be concentrated on your thoughts and beliefs in order to change the results in your life. This will certainly feel, at first, like you got the cart before the horse, but this difference in mindset-driven achievement will make all the difference.

A CASE IN POINT

In 1975, there was a research study performed at Stanford University. A group of undergraduate students were given pairs of suicide notes, one of which had been made up and composed by a writer and one which was written by someone who had attempted to take their own life. The students were asked to read the notes and distinguish which was the real note and which was the fake.

Some students found out that they were very good at the task. Out of 25 pairs of notes, they correctly identified the genuine notes 24 times. Other students discovered that they were useless at identifying the real note, finding the genuine letter only 10 out of 25 times.

In reality, the whole thing was a setup. Though half the notes were real, all the *scores* were fictitious. Those who had been told they were very good at the task and almost always right, were, in fact, no better at discerning the genuine note than those who were told they were mostly wrong.

In the second half of the study, the students were told about the deception. They were informed that their scores were fabricated and that the real purpose of the experiment was to gauge their reactions to thinking they were right or wrong. Then the students were asked to guess how many suicide letters they had actually identified correctly and how many they thought an average student would get right.

Then something fascinating occurred.

The students in the "high-score group" estimated that they had done very well—significantly better than an average student might identify—even though they had just been informed that they had no logical basis for believing this.

At the same time, the students who were assigned to the "lower-score group" estimated that they had performed notably worse than an average student might—an assumption that was just as unfounded.

Even though each student knew that their original scores were fabricated, their belief about those first results had taken hold in their minds and affected their thinking about their abilities to correctly identify a real note.

In their findings, the researchers noted, "Even after the evidence for their beliefs has been totally refuted, people fail to make appropriate revisions in those beliefs. Once formed, impressions are remarkably perseverant."

Do you see what this means? It means that mindset is more powerful than fact. It means that you can believe whatever you want. And when you believe something (either positive or negative) it will impact how you see yourself and your abilities! It means that having the *mindset* that you are qualified is the biggest determining factor in whether or not you *are* qualified.

By using the power of your thoughts, you can change how you feel and then use those feelings to achieve anything you want. If you want positive emotion driving your actions, you simply need to determine what thought will give you the feeling you need and then practice thinking that thought.

Keep in mind that mindsets can be persistent. This means that once we purposefully change our thoughts to generate the new feelings we want, we will need to consistently redirect our thoughts to that the new thought until it becomes our default mindset. (We will talk about this more in the next chapter.) Once our qualified mindset is in place, we can put it to work over and over again to create the results we want in our lives.

EXERCISES TO CHANGE YOUR MINDSET

1. Fill out the table and see how your thoughts are creating your results. Start at the bottom of the table by inserting a current undesired result and, next to it, the result you actually want. Then work your way backward on each side of the chart, until you arrive at the thoughts that create all of it.

CURRENT OUTCOME	DESIRED OUTCOME
Current Thought:	Thought:
Current Feeling:	Feeling:
Current Action (or Inaction):	Action:
Current Result:	Result:

28

In 1994, Magno Santos was a young married man living in Sao Paolo, Brazil. He had a wife and a new daughter and he worked hard at two different jobs to provide for them. He worked nights at the Sao Paolo airport at a rental car counter, helping travelers get transportation when they landed in the city. At six in the morning, he would head home and sleep for a few hours before getting on his motorcycle and heading to his second job where he picked up checks for the banks. He had a route that he would drive during rush hour, stopping at 10 different banks along the way, putting all the collected checks from the day's transactions into a large backpack, and delivering them to the central bank in downtown Sao Paolo for processing.

"One night, I was at work at the airport and a gentleman asked me to help him fill out his boarding pass and I saw that he was flying to the United States. I asked him, 'What are you going to do in the United States?' He told me, 'I'm gonna go there and work in a pizza place making pizza.'"

Magno asked him, "Do you speak English?" He didn't.

Magno asked him, "Do you read or write in English?" He didn't. In fact, he couldn't even read or write in his native Portuguese.

Then Magno asked him, "How much will they pay you to do that?" The man answered, "$1000 a month."

Magno thought the man was kidding. $1000 a month was a fortune!

Magno went home excited and told his wife about the man he had met. "He doesn't know how to read or write in Portuguese, let alone English. He can't speak any English. And he's still going to make more money than I do here, working two jobs and risking my life on the motorcycle. Can you imagine what I could do there? $1000 a month delivering pizza!"

That was the trigger.

This thought, that he could make $1000 a month delivering pizzas, caused Magno Santos to take action. That thought created a feeling of possibility and excitement. After that thought, nothing would ever be the same for him.

With this thought fueling him, Magno went into action. He sold everything he had. He sold their car, their furniture, the baby's crib, the house. Everything he could sell, he did, in order to buy the tickets to get to America. They boarded the plane with $200 left in their pockets and flew to Miami. When they landed, Magno quickly realized that he didn't even know enough English to order food. In America, Magno was even unqualified to buy a cheeseburger.

From there they flew to Salt Lake City to stay with Magno's sister. It was November 24, 1994, the day after Thanksgiving. There was snow on the ground, and Magno described it as "enchantingly beautiful." They had made it. The thought of what was possible had completely altered Magno's mindset. This seismic shift propelled Magno to action and resulted in a dramatic change in his circumstances, but it all began as an idea in his mind.

CHAPTER 3

BELIEF IN ACTION

"We are what we believe we are."

-C.S. Lewis

Now that we have examined mindset and its crucial role in our success, let's look at the way that a different belief system can create different results in our lives. Changing our thoughts and adjusting our mindset about our qualifications and abilities is the first step. Thinking those thoughts over and over again creates a belief system. When we can truly believe in our ability to accomplish our goals and achieve the things we want, *all* our actions become more powerful.

I have recently seen this play out in a very remarkable way. I volunteer as a Court-Appointed Special Advocate (CASA) in my community. In this position, I work with children in the foster care system. While the foster care system is set up to protect children, it actually doesn't operate with the child at the forefront. This isn't deliberate, but terminating the rights of a parent is, rightly, a very serious thing.

Consequently, the courts must always consider the rights of the parents ahead of anything involving the children, with the only exception being the child's immediate safety. This frequently leaves children lost in the system. In an attempt to mitigate this damage, the courts created the volunteer position of a CASA, whose sole job is to advocate in the best interest of the children.

My job as a special advocate is to determine the best situation for the child or children involved and give my recommendations to the court and judge. Additionally, a child may have serious trauma and a CASA advocates for their needs as well as any care or support they may require medically, therapeutically, or educationally.

Over the last couple of years, I have had the opportunity to work with a five-year-old boy named Christian and his half-brother, who is still a baby. Christian is a bright, caring child, but struggled in foster care despite being placed with a good family. The foster family provided structure and security and were set up so that they could eventually adopt him if the case went that way.

As I got involved, and learned the whole situation, I could see that what would be best for Christian was the care and love of his mother. Despite the worthiness of the foster family, Christian was still having a hard time in placement and was dealing with abandonment and anger issues. The foster family was trying to manage their expectations of Christian compared to their biological son and Christian was struggling to cope.

Christian's mother, Christina, due to severe addiction, had relinquished custody of him to his father when he was a baby. Fortunately, by the time Christian arrived in the foster care system, his mother was tentatively sticking a toe into recovery. I could see her potential and I could see that it would be best for Christian to be with his mother if she could continue down this path of recovery. Only she could love him and care for him the way he needed. She was the perfect person to do it, and Christian needed her.

But Christina was a product of the foster care system herself. She went into the system at the age of 13, bouncing into and running away from one group home after another. For a period of time she lived on the streets. She regularly self-medicated with drugs to deal with her pain and soon was heavily addicted to meth. At the age of 17, she was put in juvenile detention because the system just didn't have any resources to deal with her. She didn't graduate from high school and, additionally, acquired a felony along the way.

Although Christina had started her road to recovery shortly before Christian came into care, she had a long way to go and didn't believe in her ability to be a good mother. She didn't think she could do what was necessary to care for her boys and provide a home for them. She felt utterly unqualified to take care of her children and give them the life she wanted them to have.

I could see that the place to make a difference in this situation was to spend my energy investing in her. Christina needed someone to believe in her so that she could start to believe in herself. She needed someone to show her that she had everything she needed inside of her to take care of her children, to provide them with a beautiful life. She needed to see that she could do a better job mothering them than anyone else on the planet. In fact, she could be the best in the world at the one thing that mattered most in the lives of her children. She needed to believe that she was worth investing in and that she was both incredibly capable and completely qualified to be her boys' best caregiver.

I believed in her whole-heartedly and told her so until she could begin to believe it herself. I told her that *she* was what Christian needed and no one could replace her. As her mind started to think those positive thoughts over and over again, it made a dramatic difference.

What has happened in Christina's life, solely as a result of changing her thoughts, has been miraculous. She fought hard for herself, her recovery, her boys, and has reached over three years of sobriety and gained full custody of her children. She earned her GED, holds a part-time job, and enrolled in college.

(You should have seen how proud she was the day that she passed the college entrance exam.) Best of all, her boys are happy and well-adjusted and she is mothering them beautifully. She gets up early with them, keeps a clean and orderly house, provides stability, love and structure—she is truly an amazing mother.

So, what is the big take away? Circumstances mean nothing! Nothing about Christina's backstory changed. She was still a girl who grew up in the foster care system and dropped out of high school. She was still a girl who had babies young and developed a very bad drug habit. She still had pain and trauma and abandonment. She still had lived some very degrading years on the street. The *only* thing that changed was her thoughts about herself, and that in turn *changed every result she was getting in her life*. Lack of belief was the only obstacle to capacity. And she overcame it by believing exactly what she wanted to.

To watch the transformation that can happen through the power of a thought, a belief, deeply rooted, has been an incredible experience and I am glad to have witnessed it firsthand. She is an inspiration in every way. The road that she had to travel was (and still is) daunting. She has plans to help others who find themselves in similar situations as herself. The work she wants to do requires a master's degree. That is a lot of school for a single mother, but I have no doubt she will achieve her goal, because she now believes deeply in herself and her abilities.

We all have thoughts that are keeping us from achieving what we want in our lives—thoughts preventing us from starting our own business, writing that book, earning seven figures, running a marathon. We all have excuses. Christina had a long, valid list of them. But none of these beliefs are permanent or required, and we always have the option of believing something completely different in order to overcome or accomplish anything.

terrible at generating leads) comes up, you simply redirect to your new thought. Then do it over and over again until it becomes a belief. Your capacity will increase progressively as you stair-step your way to the culminating, powerful thought you want.

All of our achievement hinges on our ability to direct our thoughts. From our intentional thoughts come positive feelings that will drive our action and change our results. As we purposefully direct our thoughts to useful, empowering ones over and over again we change our fundamental belief systems.

Whether we are the CEO of a Fortune 500 company or the single mom of two incredible boys, those beliefs have the capacity to completely alter our lives. Remarkably, that untapped potential resides within each of us simply waiting to be accessed through the power of our minds.

Once we examine our mindset and create a new belief system about our qualifications and abilities, we are then ready to begin examining other characteristics that will play a key role in our success.

EXERCISES TO CHANGE BELIEF

What could you accomplish by changing the thoughts you have about your own abilities or adjusting your thoughts about your "impossible" goals? What if the *only* thing holding you back from making progress is your own mind? What thought would you change if you knew that for sure?

Write down your answers for the following questions.

1. Think about one of your goals that you aren't achieving. What is your current unhelpful belief about your ability to achieve that goal?

2. What is the exact opposite of this thought?

3. Imagine what it would be like to believe this new thought. What would you feel and how would you act if you completely believed this new thought? What would you do differently?

4. Find 5 pieces of evidence for why this new thought is true.

5. Every morning and every night write this new thought down and say it out loud to yourself. Scan your day looking for more evidence that it is true.

6. Any time the old thought comes into your mind, gently remind yourself, *I used to think that, but I no longer believe that because* _____ *(insert new thought)* _____.

7. Note: If you get stuck on #5 and can't believe the new thought, create a ladder by using words like "yet" "possible" "I'd like to believe the thought..." etc. Work your way methodically towards the new thought, doing the exercises above with each consecutive ladder thought.

Magno had made it to America. And now he had a car. But it turned out that getting a car was only half of the necessary prerequisites Magno needed to be able to deliver pizzas. The job was more than just moving a pizza from one place to another. It was actually moving a pizza from one place to another very specific place.

The owner of the restaurant just assumed that Magno knew what he was doing. But Magno was new to America and new to Salt Lake City, and he had no understanding of local directions or street names or the way the neighborhoods were laid out. Magno had a pizza and an address, but he had no idea what any of it meant. He just knew that guys who deliver pizzas make $1000 a month. What else was there to know?

Undeterred by his lack of understanding or qualification, Magno took his first pizza with address in hand and drove around looking for the house. It took him two hours to deliver the pizza.

He said, "I was looking at a map but it was night and it was dark, and so I got to the house very, very late. By then, they had called another pizza place. And they said, 'No, we don't want your pizza. Take it back.' Then I had to bring the pizza back to my boss and he said, 'Are you trying to break me? How am I going to make money if you can't deliver the pizzas?'"

Though understandably frustrated and upset, Magno's boss gave him another chance. Magno's wife told him he just needed to ask for directions, but Magno said, "No, I don't need to ask, I need to know." He bought a map of the area. Again he thought, "If they can know it, I can know it. I have a map and a car. I can figure this out."

Magno began memorizing the map, making sense of the streets, and working to know for himself. He started with the knowledge he had, which wasn't much, and he went from there.

41

"I just kept studying the map," Magno said, "I would be late with the pizza, the guy would be mad, but then I learned."

Magno eventually succeeded in learning the map and was able to deliver hot pizza night after night to finally achieve his goal. He said, "I was making $1000 a month, so that was good. But I quickly realized that $1000 isn't going to get you much here in the United States."

So Magno started asking around about jobs that paid better than pizza delivery and someone mentioned construction. Just like delivering pizzas in a foreign country, Magno knew nothing about construction. But he decided it didn't matter. He could learn. Again, he thought, "If they can know it, I can know it." He just started where he was and moved forward.

Magno told the construction manager, "I can start now."

"Do you have your tools?"

Magno said, "What tools?"

The manager gave him a list of tools. Magno asked his brother-in-law to help him read the list. "It was a hammer, it was a compass, a tool belt, other things. So, I got the tools, and the next day I start working with brand new tools."

The job they gave Magno was to carry wood and move building materials from one area of the construction site to another. "They would say, 'Two-by-four,' and I didn't know what they meant. So, I got a notebook and wrote it down. And then I measured and figured out, 'Oh, it's two inches by four inches,' and then I started learning about wood and nails and plywood and nail guns. Later on, I started doing more carpentry work and they allowed me to use the nail gun and do more things."

Magno said, "I was happy working there because it was making $7 an hour, so that was a very good job. Every two weeks, we got a paycheck and with that it allowed us to move out of my sister's house. It was amazing."

It had been six months since the Santos' had arrived in America. They had an apartment and a car and a job. Whatever Magno didn't know he learned. In every case, he started where he was and worked from there. He shoveled snow until he could make pizzas. He made pizzas until he could deliver them. He delivered pizzas until he could move 2x4s around a construction site. He moved 2x4s until he could do carpentry work. In every case, he didn't wait to know more or become qualified. He just started where he was and his skills came along with him.

CHAPTER 4

FAKE IT 'TIL YOU MAKE IT

"What e're thou art, act well thy part."
-Gaelic proverb

"Fake it 'til you make it" is a phrase that elicits strong feelings for many people. In a world full of so-called experts, social media stars, and overnight authorities on everything from marketing to meditation, it can feel like the whole world is just one big charade.

For those that feel unqualified, this is particularly troublesome and conjures up images of a disingenuous charlatan putting one over on everybody in order to make a quick buck. Rather than inspiring us with confidence, it does the opposite, making us feel insecure and anxious. This is not what I am suggesting.

It might be better to say: begin where you are. It is less about putting on an act and more about *taking action* from exactly who you are and where you are now.

HEAVY STUFF

Nearly everything you have ever weighed, from your body to a plastic bag of tomatoes, can be traced to the existence of a single item—a metal kilogram made out of platinum and iridium that was handed to Napoleon in 1799 and has been kept, sealed, and protected in an underground vault in Paris ever since.

During the French revolution, the metric system was created in an attempt to establish measurements "for all men, for all time" rather than have them randomly determined by whatever monarchy was in power at the time. For example, one unit of length at the time was *pied du Roi* or "king's foot."

In order to establish an equitable, universal measurement system, the kilogram, an actual physical artifact, was created. It's known as the International Prototype Kilogram (IPK) and it was the standard by which the entire world's weights and scales were set and calibrated.

However, there were a few problems with the IPK, or Le Grande K, as it's known by close friends. Le Grande K was slowly losing weight. It's estimated that over the last 50 years it has lost 50 micrograms, or roughly the weight of one eyelash. More importantly, as scientific discovery has progressed, the need for more fixed concepts of measurement has become necessary.

For much of history, the earth was used as the standard measuring stick. For example, a kilogram was the weight of one cubic decimeter of water. A decimeter is a tenth of a meter. But wait...what exactly is a meter?

At one time a meter was determined to be 1/10,000,000th of the distance from the North Pole to the equator. The problem arose when scientists discovered the earth itself contracts and expands. They decided they needed more fixed constants than the earth itself. They wanted numerical and physical qualities for their measurements that were thought to be unchanging throughout the entire universe.

So, for example, the meter became the first measurement to be redefined by a constant of nature rather than a measurement of the earth. In 1960, it was determined that a meter was the distance light traveled in a vacuum in 1/299,792,458th of a second. After that, six of the other seven units of measurement followed, one after the other, all redefined by constants in nature.

The kilogram was the hold out.

James Vincent wrote, "Redefining the kilogram using universal constants has been a grueling project, involving decades of research by labs around the world; the fruits of two Nobel Prizes in quantum physics; and the construction of some of the most intricate machinery ever built. It's no small task, shoring up the foundations of reality."[2]

But on November 16, 2018, Le Grande K was officially retired, as the General Conference on Weights and Measures voted to ratify the new kilogram based on universal constants of nature. Two hundred and nineteen years after Napoleon declared, "Conquests will come and go, but this work will endure," Le Grand K's noble work came to an end.

FINALLY, THE POINT

As fascinating as all of this is, what I hope you will notice is that even though the scientific standard that the IPK provided for over 200 years had flaws and ultimately needed to be more accurate, it worked. It worked for a long time.

And, more importantly, without it working for so many years—flawed and imperfect though it was—we never could have made the scientific progress, the advances in quantum physics and

---

[2] Vincent, James. "The Kilogram is Dead; Long Live the Kilogram." The Verge. Last modified November 13, 2018. Accessed December 1, 2018. https://www.theverge.com/2018/11/13/18087002/kilogram-new-definition-kg-metric-unit-ipk-measurement.

theoretical mathematics without it. Ironically, without that original artifact, we never could have replaced it.

We needed Le Grande K to come first, in order to gain the knowledge and achieve the scientific discoveries that would eventually allow us to make it obsolete.

Too many times we are waiting to arrive before we start. Chasing some idealized version of ourselves or our leadership skills or our talents and abilities, we hold back, wanting to get it exactly right. When we do this, we are not only missing out on opportunities for development and growth, we are missing out on the *only way* to get to the person we are waiting to become.

We know this logically. No one is born throwing 98 mph fastballs. No one emerges from the womb writing Pulitzer prize-winning novels. But the fear that your work just isn't good enough yet, keeps more people from pursuing their dreams than anything else.

Waiting until you are qualified is impossible. It is only in the doing that you become qualified at all. Ira Glass summed this thought up perfectly in talking about his career as a storyteller on *This American Life,* but it applies to the pursuit of any vocation or goal:

> *"Nobody tells this to people who are beginners, I wish someone told me. All of us who do creative work, we get into it because we have good taste. But there is this gap. For the first couple years you make stuff, it's just not that good. It's trying to be good, it has potential, but it's not. But your taste, the thing that got you into the game, is still killer. And your taste is why your work disappoints you. A lot of people never get past this phase, they quit.*
>
> *Most people I know who do interesting, creative work went through years of this. We know our work doesn't*

have this special thing that we want it to have. We all go through this. And if you are just starting out or you are still in this phase, you gotta know its normal and the most important thing you can do is do a lot of work. Put yourself on a deadline so that every week you will finish one story. It is only by going through a volume of work that you will close that gap, and your work will be as good as your ambitions. It's gonna take a while. It's normal to take a while. You've just gotta fight your way through."

FIGHTING YOUR WAY THROUGH

Part of "fighting your way through," as Glass puts it, means ignoring two very real and present fears: the fear of judgment and the fear of not knowing.

The fear of judgment from ourselves or others prevents many of us from starting where we are, at our current ability or talent level, and using that starting place to leverage ourselves slowly but surely to the place where we want to be.

Judgment is a perfectly normal, neutral human response to stimuli. As human brains process information, they will naturally make an assessment about its potential value or threat level. Even as you read that last sentence, your mind was weighing its validity, its perceived value in your life, its threat to established beliefs, and how it might affect your ability to survive. All of this evaluation occurred almost instantaneously and without any conscious direction from you.

When we begin to do our work in the world, we run the risk that others will see it and make a judgment about it. Just as the IPK's existence prompted scrutiny, evaluation, and eventually criticism with people literally weighing its value and worth, anything you create, produce, build, offer, share, or advertise will be vulnerable to the same examination.

Instinctively, this awareness makes us want to wait until "it's ready," "it's perfect," or we "for sure know what we're doing."

James Wedmore, author and online entrepreneur, says this can be overcome by remembering two things:

1. They will judge you either way—You cannot stop human brains from judging. That is what they were biologically and evolutionarily designed to do. The scary, collective "they" will judge you whether or not you produce products or build your business or share your art. They will judge you for doing it and they will judge you for not.

    Delaying or postponing your production until you're sure it's right, does not actually prevent any judgment at all. The judgment is still happening. It merely stops you from making real progress on your goals and dreams.

2. Those who judge you are scared of the exact same thing— Psst. Here's a secret: All those people whose judgment you're so concerned about, are just as concerned about your judgment. We're all just terrified of the exact same thing. When you can recognize that this is a universal human fear you can accept it, acknowledge it, and get some real perspective on it.

    Those who you think are judging you and your work, don't have it figured out any more than you do. They're just trying to survive.

Understand that your brain is going to vigorously resist ignoring the judgment of others. It will persistently and doggedly remind you that "they" are watching and "they" might not approve. Remind it right back that it doesn't matter in the least.

THE GREAT UNKNOWN

The second fear you have to overcome in order to start where you are is the fear of not knowing. This, of course, is tied directly into the fear of being judged, but it's worth dissecting and examining a little further on its own.

We get conditioned early that there is just one right answer and if you don't know it, something is categorically wrong with you. Even raising your hand to ask a question or to have something clarified is a situation fraught with embarrassment and humiliation. Not knowing is seen as a kind of weakness.

This is especially true in business pursuits, where not having the right answer can make you appear inexperienced or uninformed, neither of which inspire confidence in a client or consumer. However, there is another way to think about this. In fact, it turns out that the opposite may be true: *not* knowing may be the key to finding success.

I recently heard an interview with Howard Marks, one of the co-founders and chairs of Oaktree Capital and one of the country's leading financial experts and investors. Marks maintains that thinking you already know the answer is the real weakness and leaves you vulnerable to serious errors. He said, "People should wake up in the morning and start the day by practicing, 'I don't know. I don't know.' It's a great thing to say, and not enough people say it."[3]

Rather than worrying that you don't know enough to get started, imagine the freedom and creativity you can access by admitting you don't have all the answers. There is a huge difference between a person who plays small and scared because they might be exposed as an ignorant fraud and someone who may

---

[3] Ferriss, Tim. "Howard Marks — How to Invest with Clear Thinking." *The Tim Ferriss Show*. Podcast audio. September 25, 2018. https://tim.blog/2018/09/25/howard-marks/.

not know everything but plays all out because they are 100% confident they can figure it out.

A few years ago when we were expanding our business specifically into commercial restoration jobs, I was in a meeting with a client in which they brought up several concerns that we hadn't really considered or addressed before. Instead of blustering on without concrete knowledge or accepting defeat by admitting, "We have no idea. You're probably better off going with someone with more experience," my partner sat up in his chair and said, "We've run into similar situations before and I'm sure we can find a solution."

He presented our company as having the *ability* to find the answer—as well as all the answers for any unseen problems on the job—even if we didn't have the answer right then.

As soon as we got back to the office, we gathered our team and figured out how to solve the problem. In the meantime, we made the client believe that we were more than capable of doing so and then showed them that we were.

"I don't know" makes room for creativity and collaboration. It makes space for other opinions, ideas, and input. And most importantly, it allows you to start exactly where you are, as you are, with your current skills and abilities, knowing you will gain whatever else you need along the way. You cannot be the future-knowing version, without first being where you are right now.

EVERYTHING IS FIGURE-OUT-ABLE

Jody Moore is a highly successful entrepreneur and life coach. Last year her business revenue topped $1M dollars. She believes it is possible to figure out anything you need to know to build your business and reach your goals.

A couple of years ago she was running her one-on-one coaching business, charging top dollar for her coaching and still had a waiting list of clients who wanted her help. She decided to make a change in her business model and offer an online membership program for her coaching, where she would then be able to coach and help hundreds of people. She met with her CFO and told him that the following year she was going to make 3X the amount of money as she had the year before.

He said, "Really? What makes you think you're going to triple your business?"

She explained her plans and her projections and where she thought she could end up. She told him that she felt confident she could reach her goal because she was really good at sales. He said, "Well, yes, you've been selling one-on-one coaching, but you're not going to be selling anymore. You're going to be marketing. And marketing's entirely different."

Initially, this caused Moore to hesitate. She said suddenly it became a real possibility that she could fail. Then she remembered that *everything* is figure-out-able.

Instead of giving up on her goal, she simply said, "Well, I guess I'm going to have to get really good at marketing then. When I believed that that was the way and that it was possible for me to get really good at marketing, I dove in and learned everything I could about marketing. I started consuming everything I could and learning from everyone I possibly could about how to market online. Today I can say that I'm really good at sales and I'm really good at marketing. You don't have to be good at something right now to create it in the future."

Along the way, Moore had to figure out how to create effective Facebook ads. She said it was intimidating. It required her to invest real money when she wasn't even sure she was doing it right. She worried that maybe she was just throwing money away.

For a long time, she told herself that she wasn't an expert at Facebook ads. She felt like she knew the basics, and she'd had a little bit of success, but she didn't feel like an expert. She said she heard herself say that over and over again, giving herself a little pass in this area of her business. Finally, one day she heard herself say it again and said, "I'm sick of not being an expert at Facebook ads and so I'm going to become an expert."

And she dove in again. "I took as many courses as I could afford and had the time to consume. I started experimenting with them, I started failing at them and making more mistakes, and today I can say 'I'm kind of an expert at Facebook ads.'"

Even if you don't know the answer yet, or know all the steps along the way, remember that everything is figure-out-able. There is a world of information out there for anybody who wants to learn it. I learned QuickBooks through online tutorials and YouTube videos. I became an expert in business leadership through coaching, books, podcasts, and trial and error. Given the desire, you can learn to be an expert in anything. Start where you are, be willing to look for answers, and then fake it 'til you make it.

FUTURE PERFECT

Just as the IPK held a place in science for over 200 years, until the new kilogram could be defined, your present self is holding a place for your future, more capable, more qualified self. Rather than disparage and scorn your perceived limited present abilities, put them to work immediately, so that someday you can access the power of your future self.

Waiting for your future self to show up fully formed without a development process would be as fruitless as waiting for the new kilogram to just magically reveal itself to the world. Imagine if everyone—from Edison to Einstein, from Pasteur to Planck—just waited for the best version of the kilogram before performing their experiments or generating their theories. The truth is, we'd wait around in the diseased dark forever.

The present you—with all your faults and not knowing and un-qualifications—is simply a placeholder for future you. And it is good enough to get today's work done, if you choose to.

EXERCISES TO REALIZE YOUR FUTURE SELF

Your current self with your current results is a placeholder for your future self and future results. Any future you have will go through this point right now. You will need to take action starting exactly where you are now. Complete the exercises below with this in mind.

1. Choose any area of your life. Write down one goal that you would secretly love to accomplish.

2. What excuses have you been using that have prevented you realizing this goal? List them.

3. If your primary excuse was engraved on your headstone, what would it say?

4. List at least five reasons why this excuse is only a thought and not a fact.

5. What would your future self, who has already accomplished your goal, tell you is the solution to your excuse?

While Magno was grateful for the $3 an hour increase in pay, the work at the construction job was physically demanding and miserable in the winters. He started looking around for other options and was able to get a job at Costco. He started by working outside selling hot dogs and shagging carts, all the time continuing to learn and improve his English. He remembers one day when a customer asked him for a hotdog and a "beverage." He said, "Okay," and then had to find his boss and ask, "What's a 'beverage?'"

Magno loved learning and had a rule for himself. If he didn't know, he'd ask. He memorized two phrases early on: "How do you say _____?" and "What does _____ mean?"

"Then I memorized the answers and my vocabulary began to build and build and build."

Magno liked working at Costco and they liked him. In six or eight months he was able to start working for them full-time. He moved inside the store and began stocking shelves. The salary was higher and the working conditions were better. Magno was able to get health insurance and Rosie, his wife, became pregnant with their second daughter. They bought their first house and life was really good.

Magno recalls, "Life was great. It was beautiful. It was wonderful. We had small dreams and we just took it day by day."

After working for Costco for a couple of years, Magno started to get restless and frustrated. It was very labor-intensive work and much of it seemed illogical to Magno. He said, "It felt like it had no point. One day someone would say, 'Put this pallet here,' then the next day they'd ask you to move the pallet over there instead. Why? Just because somebody told me to? I kept thinking, 'Why am I doing this job? What is the purpose of doing this?'"

Magno started to desire a higher purpose in his life, something beyond the "small dream."

About this time, Magno stopped by the local mall on the way home from work one day. Someone there asked him to take a survey. It was an aptitude test to see what kinds of jobs he would be suited for. A few days later he got a letter in the mail with his results. The aptitude tests indicated that he would enjoy a career in the medical field.

Magno's neighbor worked at the University of Utah teaching anatomy to pre-med students. Magno asked him what it would take to drive an ambulance. Magno's father had been an ambulance driver in Brazil before his death and Magno had always had a desire to help others.

His neighbor explained that he would need to become an EMT but cautioned him that the job didn't pay much. Indeed, when Magno called to learn more he found out that the entry level position only paid $7 an hour and he was making almost $12 an hour at Costco. He couldn't go backwards.

While Magno was considering all of this, he happened to talk to a coworker who was going to school to be a nurse practitioner while he worked at Costco. Magno had never heard of going to school while you were working. The young man explained that he just took one or two classes at a time. This was unheard of in Brazil. To Magno, it was unimaginable.

"I thought, 'Wow! If I can take one class at a time, then I can do whatever I want. I can be a nurse, I can be a doctor, I can be whatever I want!'"

Magno now had a vision that would allow him to move his life from where it was currently—a place of "small dreams"—to a place that offered more meaning, fulfillment, and purpose. Suddenly everything opened up to him. "I knew then, if I wanted it," he said, "I just had to do it. Magno could envision his future as clearly as he could his past.

CHAPTER 5

VISION

"The future is your property."
-Dan Sullivan

One of the most distinguishing characteristics of the human brain is the ability to time travel. From your couch where you are reading this book, your mind can travel to the presentation that you have to give in a week and immediately call up an image of the room, the people, the mood in the meeting, and the feelings you will have as you stand to speak. Notice the detail your mind can create, from the water bottle sitting next to you to the opening slide of your PowerPoint presentation.

At almost the same time it can think back to your run this morning as the sun was just coming over the horizon. It can recall with vivid accuracy the temperature, the slight moisture in the air, the sounds from the road that runs past the park where you jogged. You can see what you were wearing, you can hear the music that was playing in your headphones and the steady thump, thump, thump of your heartbeat as you moved rhythmically down the path.

You can think back to when you pushed your child in the swings at that very park years ago, his pink cheeks split by a toothless grin, his head back, the breeze moving his hair back and forth with the pendulous movement of the squeaky swing. You can see his small hands gripping the metal chain as he lets his body arch with joy into the open air.

As you remember him in the swing, your mind moves forward to his wedding, just three months away, thinking about who will be there, what the invitations will look like, how he will be dressed and the slick, defined lines in his hair. You can smell his cologne, the bride's flowers, and feel the tender, bittersweet feelings of both change and blessing.

In just a moment, your brain has moved forward and back, back even farther, and then forward into a more distant future. All while you were sitting, present, reading this book in your quiet living room. The mind is in an almost constant state of time travel, moving back and forth, instantly creating both the past and the future.

For anyone with a desire to succeed, make progress in their lives, or simply to feel more qualified, one of the keys will be the ability to imagine your future and live from that future rather than the past.

While it's easy to see how being able to imagine the future gives us an evolutionary advantage—if you can plan for and anticipate the future you have a much better chance of surviving—it's important to understand that for most of us, our brains are using our past experiences to predict and construct that future. In other words, while our brains can construct the future, they usually do so using pieces and parts of the past.

If we really want to make progress, we are going to need to imagine our future using future building blocks rather than past ones. It goes back to what Henry Ford used to say about the car: "If I asked them what they wanted they would have said faster horses." In order to imagine a future that contained a car, you could not use the horse in the imagination and construction of that new future. In the same way, if we want to evolve and become a different version of ourselves, qualified and confident, we need to use totally new future building blocks, not just rearrange the past ones into a different pattern.

THE FUTURE YOU NEVER IMAGINED

In 2009, Tessie Friedli was living the life she always imagined for herself. She was married, had a one-year-old baby named Dakota, and she and her husband were building a thriving landscaping business. Everything was going as planned. But within a year, everything had changed. Her husband, a young father and entrepreneur, lost his sight because of the rare swelling of his optic nerve and was now blind.

Six months after that, two-year-old Dakota was involved in an accident, where a piece of fencing fell on him and cut off the supply of oxygen to his brain. Tessie wrote, "He went from being our perfectly healthy boy to being unable to walk, talk, eat, or even breathe on his own."

Tessie Friedli was now the wife of a blind man and the mother to a brain-injured boy. Nothing could have been further from the original vision of her life. With her imagined life in shambles around her, she surveyed the landscape ahead. Her son's future had changed. Her husband's future had changed. Everything looked different now.

Recently she wrote about how difficult creating and accepting this new future was for her. How could she be happy when the things she thought created a happy life, were no longer available? Not only that, her life now contained lots of things— therapy, surgeries, food pumps, trachs—that did not belong anywhere in the movie of her ideal life. One of these new things was a wheelchair.

"If I'm being honest," she wrote, "It took several years before we could even accept a [wheel]chair in our life. A wheelchair to others just looks like a wheelchair...but to those who find themselves having to choose "the chair" it feels permanent. It takes time to accept that this is *your* life. This chair is part of the new you.

"Dakota was two when his accident happened. Small enough to carry around and put in a stroller. We only bought our first wheelchair because he had to have it for school to ride the bus. I hated that thing and he was never in it unless he was at school."

Tessie Friedli had not imagined her future with a wheelchair in it. In all of the planning and envisioning of her life, she had never considered the possibility of her smart, active, curious son, sitting slightly slumped in a wheelchair because he couldn't walk or sit or hold himself up. How could she create a new future when it contained none of the building blocks of her past vision? Not only that, but how could she adjust to all these new pieces of reality that didn't fit anywhere in her picture of a happy life?

THE BIG LEAP

We are all in one place with a vision of where we want to get to. The problem arises because these two places do not match up. Our brains can't reconcile our reality with our future vision. Tessie was there in pain with a blind husband and a brain-injured child. She wanted to get to happily ever after. In her mind there was no way to reconcile her present situation with the future she wanted.

There is a well-rehearsed story told about Jim Carrey in this same position—standing in reality but wanting a different future. In the early 90s, Jim Carrey was a struggling actor. It was hard to get jobs and they didn't pay well. He could see where he wanted to go, but it wasn't anywhere near his current reality. In order to get to the future, he wrote himself a $10 million dollar check for "acting services rendered" and dated it for 1994. He existed in the present while expecting something different in his future. They could coexist at the same time. And in 1994, Carrey earned exactly $10 million dollars for his role in *Dumb and Dumber*.

Tessie Friedli had to make the same kind of impossible leap. She said, "I remember so clearly one night, sitting in bed crying—one of many nights I spent crying—and struggling after months and months of *really* hard days and nights. I remember wishing so badly that I could just fast forward life like 10 years! I wanted to feel happiness again and I had a hope that I would...I just couldn't see how or when that would be."

Like Carrey, though perhaps on a much more excruciating level, Tessie had a vision of what was possible, her mind just couldn't make the connection between that future moment and the place she was now. Tessie's life had irreversibly changed. Could she still create the life she wanted with her husband regardless of challenge or a change in plans? Could she have the future of her dreams?

"Sitting there that night I could see the future me, and she was happy. In ten years, I was really, genuinely happy. Suddenly, I realized I could just be her anytime I wanted. It is what we choose that determines who we are and how happy we can be. And I could choose that anytime I wanted. Since then, I am able to do a lot of things that at one point seemed impossible."

For each of us, there is a leap that we must make from our current reality to the life we want. What we need to understand is that we can't wait to make the leap until it becomes reasonable and believable and logical. We can't wait around until the circumstances indicate that now it's possible because that moment never comes. The only way we get from here to there is to make the jump even when it's impossible, incredible, and utterly unbelievable.

How do we know what future to imagine if we haven't ever been there before? Here's the truth: you get to make it up. You get to write the check for whatever date you want for whatever amount you want. You get to be your future self—whatever you want it to look like—any time you decide to.

What these stories and hundreds of others like them show us, is that we get to create whatever we want. It doesn't have to be believable, it doesn't have to be reasonable, it doesn't have to be probable or even possible. As the Queen told Alice when she protested that you can't believe impossible things, "I daresay you haven't had much practice."

People get caught up on this. They think it's "delusional" or "ridiculous" not to accept "what's real." But Byron Katie teaches that our life is just a dream—meaning, it's simply a mental construct from which we decide what's true and what's not, who we are and who we aren't, what we value and what we don't, what we believe and what we don't. You get to create whatever you want because you get to believe whatever you want. It's all a creation rather than a "reality."

Was it delusional for Tessie Friedli to think she could be happy when her husband was blind and her son was brain-injured? Was it ridiculous for Jim Carrey to think he could ever earn $10 million dollars? The delusion is only ever in our mind. Do you want to delude yourself that you are capable of anything or do you want to delude yourself that you are nothing special? What Katie is saying is that either way, it's a delusion. Pick your delusion.

FILLING IN THE FUTURE

Dr. Dennis Deaton was a successful dentist with a thriving practice and a family of nine children. He had a life, a home, a career, and a "safe future." There was nothing more to do now than be happy and enjoy his life.

But Dr. Deaton had that little voice inside him, encouraging him that he could do more. He was a gifted teacher and loved to speak and share ideas and insights. He felt the desire for a different future than the one he had once imagined and built with traditional building blocks.

He began giving seminars to other dentists to help them grow their practices and set big goals. The more he did it, the more he loved it. The business expanded and he started giving seminars on managing your mind and the power of your thoughts. He started teaching outside of the medical field and got some contracts in corporate America, including a big contract with Motorola which was based in the Phoenix area.

Dennis knew if he was going all in on his dream, it was time to make the leap. He would have to sell the dental practice he had steadily built over the years and move his large family to another state and change every aspect of his life. There would be no going back. To get to the new version of himself living in the future of his dreams, he would have to believe in impossible things.

He had a choice. He could stay in the life he had built with its steady income and predictable future, or he could listen to that other voice, the alternative future that was beckoning him simultaneously towards uncertainty and growth.

Dr. Deaton went all in. He sold his practice, packed up the house and the nine kids and arrived in a new future. It didn't all go perfectly. But over time, the vision of what he could build and what he could become in the process came into reality. Dr. Dennis Deaton is now a nationally-known speaker and thought leader with corporate clients all over the country. Thousands of people have been impacted by his message that our thoughts create our destiny—and that if we can control those, we get to have whatever future we want.

FEED THE BEAST

There is a story told about a Cherokee grandfather who taught his grandson about the power of his internal life and what he could create for himself. He likened his inner life to two wolves.

"A fight is going on inside me," he told his grandson. "It is a terrible fight between two wolves. One is evil—he is anger, sorrow, envy, regret, greed, arrogance, self-pity, guilt, resentment, inferiority, lies, false pride, superiority, and ego."

He continued, explaining, "The other is good—he is peace, joy, love, hope, serenity, humility, abundance, kindness, benevolence, compassion, truth, generosity, and faith."

Then he said, "The same fight is going on inside you—and inside every other person, too."

His grandson thought about this. "But, which wolf will win?"

His grandfather replied, "The one you feed."

This metaphor is just as applicable to the futures available to you. There is a fight going on inside you, in which two opposing futures are competing. The one future is made up of your limitations, your reservations, your inadequacies, your insecurities, and the story you tell about who you are and what you are capable of. It rejects growth and change and possibility. It shows you what's impossible and improbable and certainly out of your reach. It wants to stay safe and small and, perhaps, bored, but at least not scared.

The other future is everything you've ever wanted. It is made up of your hopes and dreams and wild fantasies. It is made up of your vision and your possibility and potential. It is full of the dreams that rise up again and again, pestering you and reminding you that you can do more, be more, feel more. It is expansive and brave and daring. It urges you to reach and try and go all in.

Every moment, every decision, every sunrise, you decide which one you'll feed. Will you continue feeding and nursing your inadequacies and insecurities? Or will you begin the practice of believing impossible things, putting all your energy into fueling the future of your dreams? As Jim Kwik pointed out, "If you argue for your limitations, you get to keep them."

PICTURE PERFECT

Sara Blakely is the founder and creator of Spanx, Inc. She has a billion-dollar business and her products are found in high-end retail stores around the world. She built her business from the ground up; she saw a problem, had an idea, and created a shapewear empire from her solution.

Blakely credits her success to a few things including embracing failure and setting high goals, but she said one of the most important keys to her accomplishments was having a vision. She said, "When I was selling copiers door-to-door, I had a very clear vision of what my life was going to be like and I was specific in that vision."[4]

Sara knew exactly what she wanted: she wanted to be self-employed, she wanted to invent a product that she could sell to lots of people, and she wanted to create a business that could be self-sustaining and keep making money even if she wasn't present. She continually pictured herself living a life with those parameters.

Blakely encourages everyone who wants to achieve big goals to create a vision and take a mental snapshot of what success looks like to you. Imagine and visualize all the details: what does your day look like, how much money do you earn, how many people

---

[4] "Spanx's Sara Blakely - Tips for Success." Video file, 3:19. YouTube. Posted by PrimeauTV, April 25, 2013. Accessed February 25, 2019. https://www.youtube.com/watch?v=ZGh-Ic9wdvI.

do you supervise, how much revenue do you generate, where do you live, what do you drive, how are you recognized in your industry? Can you picture the stages you will stand on, the boardrooms you will sit in, the meetings you will lead, the events you will attend? Whatever success means to you, create a vivid picture of it in your mind and take a snapshot.

Then, Blakely says, "Hold onto that snapshot and you will subconsciously start to make decisions that will get you there." Our brain automatically goes to work creating the future we have imagined because, remember, in the mind the future is as real as the past.

In 2015, the U.S. Women's Soccer team beat Japan 5-2 in the World Cup Championship, the first win for the U.S. Women since 1999. It was well publicized that before the game, team captain Carli Lloyd, visualized herself scoring four goals in the game.

Lloyd said, "I dreamed of and visualized playing in the World Cup final and visualized scoring four goals. It sounds pretty funny, but that's what it's all about. I think at the end of the day you can be physically strong, you can have all the tools out there, but if your mental state isn't good enough, you can't bring yourself to bigger and better things. And for me, I've just constantly been visualizing, constantly been growing confidence with each and every game and I was on a mission."[5]

Lloyd went on to score three of the five goals that secured the team's victory. She visualized it after a practice in May and created it in reality two months later in July.

---

[5] Litman, Laken. "Carli Lloyd had a vision she'd score four goals in the World Cup final." *USA Today* (Vancouver), July 6, 2015, national edition, Sports. Accessed February 25, 2019. https://ftw.usatoday.com/2015/07/ carli-lloyd-had-a-vision-shed-score-four-goals-in-the-world-cup-final.

Perhaps, the most amazing part about believing impossible things is how specific you can be in your visualization to get what you want.

There have been numerous studies regarding the power of imagery and visualization, including one in which participants were asked to play a simple sequence of piano notes every day for five consecutive days. Brain scans were performed each day to see the activity in the area of the brain connected to the finger muscles.

In the study, another group of participants were asked to simply *imagine* playing the sequence of notes, but not actually touch the piano keys.[6] Their brains were also scanned every day. There was also a control group that neither played the sequence of notes nor imagined playing them, that also underwent a daily scan.

---

[6] Pascual-Leone, A., D. Nguyet, L. G. Cohen, J. P. Brasil-Neto, A. Cammarota, and M. Hallett. "Modulation of muscle responses evoked by transcranial magnetic stimulation during the acquisition of new fine motor skills." *Journal of Neurophysiology* 74, no. 3 (September 1995): 1037-45.

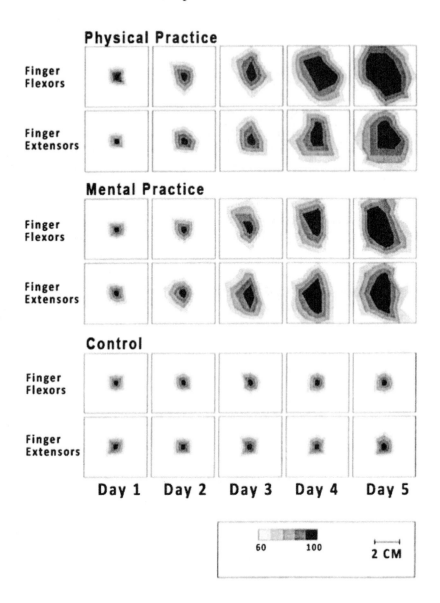

The top two rows in the image above shows the changes in brain activity for those who played the notes on a piano. The middle two rows display the brain activity changes for those who *only imagined* playing the notes. Compare both of these results with those who neither played the notes nor imagined playing the notes.

It is clearly evident that those who only imagined playing the notes created the same changes in their brain as those who actually practiced on a keyboard. Your brain does not differentiate between a real and imagined event. Whatever you can create in your mind, your brain will believe and create the neuropathways to accomplish the task.

See yourself in that future place, doing the things that you want to do. Take a picture of that future self and hold onto it. Just as Carrey, Friedli, and Blakely have proven, having a clear vision of what you want causes your brain to go to work solving the problems and obstacles between you and your future self and bringing your picture into reality.

THE FUTURE IS YOUR PROPERTY

So what is it that you want to create in your life? Do you have a specific vision for what you want? Or is it just a general, nebulous idea of "I want to be better" or "I want to feel better" or "I thought I would be better by now." Be aware that this undefined feeling of lukewarm dissatisfaction does not create a picture or a clear objective for the brain to work towards.

Too many of us think our results just happen to us. We don't steer the ship because we have no idea that it can be steered. We think the sea is setting the course, or perhaps the rest of the people we're travelling with are controlling the direction, or perhaps it's the kind of ship we're in that makes the difference. We blame our circumstances, our families, our jobs, and our bosses. We think it's the way we were raised or the quality of our education or the access we had to opportunity.

One reason we aren't getting the outcomes we want is because we don't know that we are in charge of that. We are in charge of deciding what we want (having a vision) and we are in charge of getting it.

Kevin and Keith Hanson are a pair of brothers, a couple of track geeks, that owned a couple of running-shoe stores in Detroit. They decided to start a running club to get people excited about long distance running. "There weren't enough successful American runners in the 1990s. We figured we should do something about it. Our whole idea was to get back to group training."

The Hansons had a vision for their business and their sport. They could see what they wanted for the running community and for themselves. And they got busy building that future on their own terms. The Hansons Running Shops were not just selling shoes. Their mission, as they saw it, was to sell the fun of running. They created opportunities to promote that fun—group runs, running camps, marathon clinics. They followed local runners and watched the school cross-country teams in the cities where their shops were located.

I love what Keith Hanson said when he was asked about their success, "Sometimes other shop owners will complain to me that running's down in their area. And I think, 'You do know you're in charge of that, right?'"[7]

The Hansons are in charge of their business. They take responsibility for all of it—even the general running interest in their community and the deterrent Michigan winters. It's all up to them.

At first glance, that philosophy may seem overwhelming. But the opposite is true. Taking responsibility for the creation of your future is empowering. It's up to you and no one else. And, good

---

[7] Barcott, Bruce. "She Can Do It!" Runner's World. Last modified December 28, 2011. Accessed January 25, 2019. https://www.runnersworld.com/races-places/a20805033/desiree-davila-can-do-it/.

news, it turns out that you are the one and only thing you can actually control.

What would happen in your future if you adopted this thought: You do know you're in charge of that, right? This is what I ask myself every time I have a vision of what I can become, every time that voice inside me whispers that something else is possible. When my brain resists the growth and tells me it can't be done, I remind myself, "Of course I can; I'm in charge of that."

I'm in charge of the vision for my life and I'm in charge of the outcomes. The future is your property. You own all of it.

When we finally stop coddling and nurturing the unqualified, insecure side of ourselves that wants to abdicate this responsibility, and start taking counsel from the part of us that can believe impossible things, that's when things can really start to change. It is only then that a new future is created and becomes available to step into.

EXERCISES TO EXPAND YOUR VISION

1. Starting with a blank slate, imagine the future you want. What does success look like to you?

   What do you do every day? Where do you live? How much do you earn? What contributions do you make in your industry? What problems do you solve? Get as specific as possible.

   A word of caution: If I asked you to envision your dream house, you probably wouldn't start with your current house and just add an extra wing or two more bathrooms. You would start from scratch, creating everything exactly as you want it. In the same way, as you envision your future success, don't take your past building blocks with you unless they are truly a part of your ideal future. Start from scratch and create a vision for exactly what you want.

2. Take a snapshot of that future and record your vision in writing. Make the description as vivid and detailed as possible.

3. Spend a few minutes every day visualizing your future so that your mind can go to work believing it and then creating it.

On the day Magno learned that he could take one class at a time, he went straight from his shift at Costco to the local community college to find out what he had to do to enroll. The first thing he had to do was pass an entrance exam.

Magno paid $15 to take the test and flunked it. His English wasn't good enough. Even Magno's math skills were barely passable. He had only attended school through the eighth grade in Brazil before his father died.

The college recommended that Magno take some ESL classes and then come back and try again. Instead, Magno got a newspaper subscription. Every day he read the paper, translating and transcribing it as he went.

Then the Santos' second daughter was born. Magno said, "As hard as it was going to be to go to school and pay for school and work while I was doing it, I knew that if I worked at it, by the time my second daughter was entering the first grade, I could be graduating. It was the price I was willing to pay."

But first Magno had to pass the entrance exam. He worked for three months using the newspaper to improve his English and passed the exam. "I passed at the lowest level of English and the lowest level of math, but I was in. I started taking one class at a time."

As much sacrifice as it required, Magno exercised his grit and went to work. Day in and day out, starting his shift at Costco at 4:30 in the morning and then going to class and then going home to study as hard as he could. Magno had lots of ground to make up and none of it was easy.

Magno remembers, "I flunked many classes. I remember sitting in biology class and it was in a big auditorium. I was sitting all the way in the back and the professor started talking about "offspring." In my head I thought, 'What's off spring?' I thought that he must be talking about summer because spring came before summer and this was just off spring. There we were talking about Darwin and I wondered, 'What does summer have to do with it?'"

Despite the uncomfortable, disheartening growth curve he faced, Magno kept going doggedly towards his goal. Speaking of the difficult work, he said, "I got used to it, you know. You learn every day and you keep going."

Eventually, one or two classes at a time, Magno finally finished all his prerequisites to apply for a nursing degree.

The process to passing his prerequisites took years and years of tremendous effort. It would have been so easy to quit, to just settle back into the small dream and take the easier way. But Magno Santos had grit—he was okay with discomfort if it was going to get him where he wanted to be.

CHAPTER 6

GRIT

"Grit is not just a simple elbow-grease term for rugged persistence. It is an often invisible display of endurance that lets you stay in an uncomfortable place, work hard to improve upon a given interest and do it again and again."

-Sarah Lewis

On June 1st of 2018, Ross Edgely dove into the ocean off the coast of Great Britain with a monumental goal in front of him. He was making an attempt to swim 2000 miles around the mainland coast of the entire British isles.

The feat required him to be in the water twelve to fourteen hours a day, swimming roughly the equivalent length of the English Channel every single day. Along the journey, Edgely faced enormous obstacles including jellyfish swarms, powerful currents, gale-force winds, crushing waves, ice-cold water, night swims, and a disintegrating tongue due to "salt mouth."

In fact, most of the 15,000 calories Edgely had to consume every day had to be liquified and poured into a cake piping bag and then squeezed into his mouth because his tongue and throat suffered so much damage from the sea water.

When Edgely entered the water that summer day, his goal was to circumnavigate Great Britain in less than a hundred days. When all was said and done, Edgely made it back to the starting point, having swam 1,798 miles, roughly the distance from London to Moscow, in 157 days—a full eight weeks longer than he planned. Because of strong currents and fierce tides, there were grueling portions of the swim where he actually made negative progress and finished the day behind where he started it.

Does this sound achingly familiar to anyone?

In addition to a rotting tongue, Edgely experienced extreme chafing and salt sores from his wetsuit and would often wake with open wounds fused to his sheets. He said the darkest moment of the swim came during a night swim off the coast of Scotland in the Gulf of Corryvrecken whirlpool. In the middle of the world's third-largest whirlpool, a giant jellyfish attached itself to Edgely's face for 30 minutes. It was the real-life version of Scotland's infamous Loch Ness monster.

He said, "The sting was searing into my skin; it wrapped around my goggles. This fat, giant jellyfish of Scotland and its tentacle had been slapping me in the face for half an hour through a giant whirlpool. It was brutal but you couldn't stop."[8]

By the time Ross Edgely reached the finish line in Margate in early November, he had a nasty open neck wound from the top of his wetsuit's relentless rubbing (talk about rubbing salt in the wound!), a suspected torn shoulder from nearly 2.5 million strokes in the open ocean, and feet and leg muscles that had atrophied so much he could no longer walk without extreme difficulty.

Spending so many hours in sea water every day caused additional complications, creating what is effectively "trench foot," where the skin on his hands and feet became rotted by the

---

[8] Halliday, Josh. "'It was brutal': Ross Edgley completes 157-day swim around Britain." *The Guardian*, November 4, 2018, UK News. Accessed December 18, 2019. https://www.theguardian.com/uk-news/2018/nov/04/it-was-brutal-ross-edgley-completes-157-day-swim-around-britain.

elements. Edgely also faced the real threat of hypothermia; the severe cold of the water, 60 degrees Fahrenheit, left him shaking uncontrollably when he returned to the boat.

"Setting out, I knew [it] would be the hardest thing I've ever attempted. I was very naïve at the start, and there were moments where I really did begin to question myself," Edgely admitted. "Hands down the hardest thing on so many levels: physical, mental. I felt a fatigue that I've never felt before. The neurotransmitters in the brain were just like 'What are you doing?'"

HELLO DARKNESS, MY OLD FRIEND

In the face of so much physical and mental pain, it makes you wonder why Edgely kept going. How did he swim stroke after stroke, when no one was watching, along a quiet, forlorn coast in the middle of the North Sea? How did he jump back into the freezing water, night after night, with only the stars to witness his bravery? How did he pull his wetsuit back on again and again, over the sores under his armpits and zip it up tight to rub and dig relentlessly against the open wound on his neck? How did he get back in the water when he had only made negative progress for three days straight? How, in those quiet, painful moments, did he overcome his own brain?

The answer is that Ross Edgely is completely comfortable with discomfort. In one interview he noted that the mental acceptance of constant discomfort is exactly what allowed him to reach his goal. "I'm constantly in the cold water or in my bed, which is rocking side to side in the waves, but as long as you make peace with that fact, the Great British Swim becomes possible."

The willingness to stay in discomfort for extended periods of time is the essence of grit. It also happens to be an essential key to achieving anything you want.

Grit is far more than determination or perseverance or hard work. It is all of these things in the presence of discomfort for as long as it takes, especially when there is no one there to watch or cheer or admire. Grit is the mental power required to make the lonely painful push through the uncomfortable and sometimes excruciating moments that precede achievement of any kind.

THE REAL OBSTACLE

In order to maximize our chances for survival, the brain was evolutionarily designed to avoid pain, seek pleasure, and conserve energy. While these objectives may have been extremely useful in preserving our species initially—watch out for danger, eat and procreate, save energy to fight or flee—these automatic responses are no longer nearly as necessary or useful as they once were.

While the clear and present threats to our survival have dramatically decreased, our brains are still working subconsciously from the same motivational triad. In many cases, this means that those instincts that once kept us alive are now the very things holding us back. When you are uncomfortable, the brain alerts you that something has gone terribly wrong and something needs to change immediately. Staying in discomfort means directly confronting all three of these deeply ingrained, biological mechanisms.

First, when you choose discomfort you are purposely embracing rather than avoiding pain. Next, you are eschewing immediate pleasure in exchange for a long-term reward. And finally, you are spending considerable amounts of energy overcoming your instincts, thinking new thoughts, and forging new neuropathways rather than thinking what you've always thought.

When you exercise true grit, you are doing exactly the opposite of what the brain is biologically wired to do. And if your brain is working properly, it's going to freak out. Death is imminent! When you stay in discomfort on purpose, you are, in every way, working against your own brain.

When you understand this, you can see what Ross Edgely was really up against. It wasn't the 10-foot swells or the treacherous undercurrents, or even the 37 brutal jellyfish stings. It was his own brain, constantly nudging him to stop, begging him for rest, tempting him to get out of the cold, pleading with him not to get back in the salt water, screaming at him to just let up.

His arms and his shoulders and his feet and his face and his neck and his armpits—all of them—were sending signal after signal that something was wrong, and the brain responded to all that pain and discomfort with thoughts; they started as a little chatter, then serious, authoritative commands, and then full-on alarm bells: *This is crazy. What are you doing? This was a terrible idea. No one will know if you quit. How did you think this was even possible? You're doing permanent damage to your body. You could die out here. You are definitely going to die out here.*

And on and on and on. For 157 days, 1798 miles, and 2.5 million strokes.

THE CASE FOR PAIN

No matter what your goals are—make a million dollars, lose forty pounds, become a morning person, run a marathon, write a book, earn your doctorate, 10X your business, become an industry leader—discomfort is the price you have to be willing to pay to achieve it.

Your pleasure-seeking, pain-avoiding, energy-conserving brain is going to reject this idea. It's going to look around for examples of people who did all of the above without really even trying. Clearly, success just fell into their lap.

Your brain will try to sell you on the idea that everything doesn't have to be this hard, that life was meant to be enjoyed, that discomfort is just the currency the foolish people pay. There has to be an easier way. When you indulge your brain and entertain this kind of thinking, you are wasting time. Instead of working on your goal, your brain spends its energy finding evidence to support the idea that the whole endeavor should be easy. *Why isn't this easy? Some people are just lucky. I can't catch a break.*

The truth is a primary reason any of us have not achieved what we want—from weight loss to building our businesses to improving our relationships—is that we have *chosen not to be uncomfortable*. We have opted for ease over achievement.

You'll never see a diet plan that pitches, "Our plan is a lot of discomfort followed by more discomfort followed by some uneasiness and some annoyance followed by a bit of distress and restlessness, followed by a lifetime of discipline to eat right and keep yourself at your goal weight." It turns out that discomfort is not a big seller.

But it is the solution.

Change is uncomfortable. Risking failure and exposing yourself to rejection is uncomfortable. Ignoring the urges and nudges and signals from the brain is uncomfortable. But, the sooner you embrace the fact that pain and discomfort are a necessary part of achieving any goal, the sooner you "make peace" with pain, as Edgely says, the sooner you can release your resistance and move your energy towards actual achievement.

Mark Twight spent years doing difficult alpine climbs of some of the world's most unforgiving mountain peaks. He wrote about the connection between discomfort and achieving his goals:

Grit

> *"I trained. I punished myself. I thought making myself suffer on a day-to-day basis would prepare me for climbing hard at high altitude. I slept on the floor. I carried ice in my bare hands. I beat them against the concrete just to see if I could handle it. I never missed an opportunity to train. I ran stairs until I vomited, then ran more. I ruined relationships to get used to the feeling of failure and sacrifice. I trained in the gym on an empty diet to learn how far I could push myself without food or water. I subdued my fears. I was ready for anything."[9]*

You might not agree with his methods, and in some instances, they are rather extreme, but Twight, like Edgely, embraced the discomfort. He did not spend his energy wishing it wasn't going to be hard or resisting the discomfort that was necessary for achievement. Instead he accepted and anticipated the pain, looked for ways to practice feeling discomfort on a regular basis, exercised his grit, and reached his goals.

DISSECTING DISCOMFORT

It turns out that if you have a desire to grow and evolve and are not acting on it, you are already in discomfort. You live with a constant nagging feeling, a dissatisfaction with your life, a persistent unhappiness from not meeting your potential. You are perpetually carrying the discomfort of wasted days and self-contempt.

If you are a religious person like me, you view this as a God-given gift to each of us. A call to reach for something higher, to become better, to expand, to grow and to stretch. But, whatever your spiritual persuasion, that discomfort of unmet potential is real. Twight called it "the infected loneliness that comes at the end of every misspent day [when] I knew I could do better."

---

[9] Twight, Mark. *Kiss or Kill: Confessions of a Serial Climber*. N.p.: Mountaineers Books, 2002.

Even in the face of this, your brain will try to talk you out of your goal. It will spend hours persistently telling you that it's too hard, that it's not worth it, there are too many obstacles to overcome, you can begin tomorrow, and on and on. The bottom line is that you have a choice. You can listen to the whine of your brain in the middle of discomfort, or you can listen to the litany of regrets from not responding to that divine urging to become a higher version of yourself.

As humans, we do our best to ignore relentless discomfort by buffering away these feelings by overeating or over drinking or losing ourselves for hours in social media or binge-watching Netflix or any variety of other numbing agents. These are false pleasures; something to simply keep your brain distracted from the gnawing discomfort of stagnation.

Here's the truth: there is discomfort either way. You either have the discomfort of staying where you are, living your life exactly as it is, or you have the discomfort of fear and fatigue and hunger and rejection and loss and even failure as you work towards your goals. The only difference is that if you endure the latter discomfort, if you exercise your grit and stay in the discomfort of growth, you also have achievement waiting inevitably at the other side of all that discomfort.

For those who want more from themselves and from their lives, the key is to harness your grit and choose the discomfort of growth. For those who want to achieve greatness and push their own personal limits, the discomfort of settling or ease is simply intolerable.

Before Ross Edgely swam around Great Britain, he attempted to swim from Martinique to St. Lucia in the Caribbean with a 100 lb. tree trunk tied to him. Because powerful currents took him off course he had to abandon the swim without reaching the island and it haunted him afterwards. Though he estimates he swam more than the distance required, the direction was off and he never reached land.

Edgely's perceived failure created enough discomfort for him that he was determined to do something even harder. Thus, the Great British Swim was born. The swim around the British mainland was about as demanding and uncomfortable as any goal ever set, but it was still less uncomfortable than living with his unfinished attempt in the Caribbean.

Dissecting the discomfort in your own life allows you to make a conscious choice. Do you want the restless discomfort of living a life of unfulfilled dreams or do you want the rigorous discomfort that is accompanied inseparably and inextricably by achievement? Grit is the defining trait that separates the two. The choice is always yours.

DISCOMFORT IN THE DESERT

I've run a few ultra-marathons in my life, across the quiet, simmering deserts of Arizona and southern California. I know something of the way your mind can work against you when your body is in pain; the way it coaxes and coddles and creates arguments for stopping, for easing up, for quitting whenever the going gets rough. And then there are moments when that coaxing transitions into downright screaming: *You're going to die.*

Your mind works against you when the alarm goes off at 3:45 am so you can get 20 miles in before the day starts. Your mind rebels vehemently 39 km into a 50 km race with the next water station a full eight kilometers away. When the sun is high, your salt levels are low, and you are at the base of a hill aptly named "King Kong," there is so much internal, mental clamor you can't even hear yourself breathe. *You're going to die.*

The greatest knowledge that I gained from these races, is that it's not the actual race days that require the heroic efforts. It is having the grit to make it to the starting line. It's the hours upon hours of unremarkable and unnoticed training sessions. It's learning to endure the endless miles of exertion in the scorching Arizona summer. It is those grueling back-to-backs when you run 18 miles one morning just to follow it up with a 20-miler the next. It's when your legs feel like lead and you're out in the middle of nowhere with no audience. That's when the voice screams the loudest: *WHY? Give me one reason why you are doing this VOLUNTARILY?*

In an ultra-marathon across the desert, and in the dark seas of the North Atlantic, and on the sheer face of K2, there are a million different moments of truth. How bad do you want this? Just exactly how much discomfort are you willing to endure?

Really, I find that it's no different in business. The physical discomfort is simply replaced by emotional discomfort. There's enough fear and misgiving and risk involved that your mind tends to work against you, creating disaster scenarios, convincing you that failure is inevitable, talking you into staying small and settling for good enough. *You're going to die.*

But I have also found that, just as in marathons, the really good stuff, the mind-blowing success and unbelievable results, are out beyond the fear and discomfort. When I have achieved the most success, it is because I used enough grit to push past my comfortable boundaries to accomplish what was once impossible. You have to ignore your doubts, your misgivings, your "logical" thoughts, and help your team to ignore them too.

Brooke Castillo, founder of the Life Coach School, says, "Remember if you don't feel like working on your goal, that is normal. Discomfort is the currency of your dreams." There is always a price for what we want—whether it's growing our business, raising the standards of excellence in our product, improving the productivity of our teams, or starting a new venture. This price, inevitably, is discomfort, which creates mental pushback and resistance and growing pains.

But the discomfort is the very thing that makes us better as we progress and is the way—the only way—to get what we want. You want incredible results? Get good at discomfort. You want to achieve your dreams? Get good at discomfort. You want the impossible? Get really, really good at discomfort.

Bottom line: the more grit you can maintain and exercise through extended periods of discomfort, the closer you will get to achieving everything you want in your life.

EXERCISES TO GROW GRIT

We get good at whatever we practice. Choose any one of these exercises to grow your grit by improving your ability to experience and endure discomfort. As you do them, pay attention and notice the thoughts that come up. *Why are we doing this? This is stupid. This can wait until later. It's not worth it. We're going to die.* Become fascinated by your brain's predisposition to avoid discomfort. That awareness alone will increase your supply of grit.

1. Take cold showers. Set a timer and see how long you can stay in the shower. Start slowly and increase the amount of time in the cold shower every day.

2. Fast regularly. Set a regular time, monthly, to fast from sun-up to sun-down. Let your body experience hunger and purposefully ignore the brain's insistent signals to eat.

3. Identify and eliminate your most well-used numbing agents. What do you do when you don't want to do what you need to? What do you do when you're restless, bored, or uncomfortable? Once you identify your buffers, select one to eliminate by deciding ahead of time exactly when you will do the activity and stick to your boundaries.

   For example, if you numb with social media, decide ahead of time that you will check it on Friday night from 6-7. Ignore the cues from your brain to check social media at any other time. Watch your life change with every buffer you remove.

4. Sleep a night on the floor.

5. Go for a run or engage in another physically-challenging activity. Get to the point where you would normally quit and keep going.

Keep in mind that you are not engaging in discomfort to punish yourself, or start a practice of masochism, but simply to practice becoming comfortable with discomfort. These exercises allow you to direct your own mind to accept and make peace with optional pain and irritation.

Remember that it's actually all optional! Choosing to reach your goals is optional. And your mind will keep reminding you of that over and over again as you come face-to-face with your fears. By doing these exercises in "optional discomfort" ahead of time, you are training your brain to accept that you can choose discomfort—even when it's optional.

Exercising your mental power in this way will grow your grit!

Throughout Magno's journey, he faced fear at almost every point along the way. When he first arrived in a new country with only $200 and not a single word of English in his vocabulary, he discovered that he couldn't work without proper documentation. He was seized by fear. He had no way to work. He had no way to go back to Brazil. He didn't have money for a ticket home and even if he could get there, the Santos's had sold everything they owned. They had nothing to go back to.

When asked about his fears, Magno said, "Every moment is a decision. Will you choose fear or will you choose optimism? Fear won't help you solve your problems. I was always optimistic that I could figure things out."

As he thinks back on all the steps he took and the way he figured things out along the way, Magno remembers that one of the scariest moments was when he and Rosie went to buy their first house. He was terrified about the process, his financial qualifications, and all the things he still didn't know about building a life in a new country.

"I was so scared of the paperwork and so afraid of everything—the entire process—that right before we had to go sign the papers to close on the house, I got extremely sick. The fear was so severe it just took over my body."

But Magno fought through his fears one at a time to get what he wanted in his life. "There was always fear," he said. "There was fear that I wouldn't get into a nursing program after I finished my prerequisites. There was fear I wouldn't pass the nursing certification exam after all that work. There was fear at every new step. But I would say this phrase to myself: 'Be proud of how far you have come and have faith in how far you can go.' I memorized that and said it whenever the fear came up."

Magno didn't let fear and doubt get in his way—and he had plenty to choose from: fear of starvation, fear of the language, fear of getting lost, fear of inadequacy, fear of not being smart enough, fear of wasting his time and his money, fear he couldn't keep going, fear of uncertainty, fear of failure. Over and over, he had to face the monsters of doubt and discouragement in his own head, with their reminders of his lack and his deficiencies and his inadequacy.

Every moment was a decision. What would he choose? Magno continuously and purposefully decided to ignore his fears and have faith in how far he could go.

CHAPTER 7

FEAR

"Of all the liars in the world, sometimes the worst are our own fears."

— Rudyard Kipling

Alex Honnold is one of the most famous free solo climbers in the world, meaning that he scales the sheerest, most difficult rock faces on the planet without ropes or harness or even a helmet. It's just him, the rock, and a whole lot of empty space.

In June of 2017, Alex completed the most dangerous free-solo ascent in history when he climbed El Capitan in Yosemite National Park, a 3000-foot, granite wall that juts up out of the park. El Capitan is a legendary spot in the rock-climbing world. Its vertical reach stretches more than a half mile into the sky and is higher than the tallest building in the world, Burj Khalifa in Dubai. From the foot of the rock, climbers on the peak are invisible to the naked eye. Alex Honnold ascended to these heights without a single piece of safety equipment.

As he climbs, Honnold has literally no margin of error. Any climb above 50 feet is likely to be lethal, so when Alex is free soloing, he spends hours and hours in what climbers call the "Death Zone."

About Honnold's climbs, J.B. MacKinnon wrote, "On the hardest parts of some climbing routes, his fingers will have no more contact with the rock than most people have with the touchscreens of their phones, while his toes press down on edges as thin as sticks of gum."[10]

For most people, just watching a video of one of these climbs induces heart palpitations or moments of serious vertigo. Alex himself admits that watching himself on film makes his palms sweat.

ARE YOU CRAZY?

Three years before scaling El Capitan, after another impossible climb on the peaks of the Musandam Peninsula in the Persian Gulf, Honnold and some other climbers were giving a presentation at Explorer's Hall, at the headquarters of the National Geographic Society. After the presentation, a neurobiologist told one of the other climbers, pointing at Honnold, "That kid's amygdala isn't firing."

The amygdala is where the fear center is housed in the brain. It is at the very base of the brain and was one of the first parts of the brain to develop evolutionarily. It was a critical piece in our species' survival. After seeing the pictures from Alex Honnold's most recent climb, the neurobiologist concluded that something must be seriously wrong with Honnold's amygdala because he wasn't demonstrating any of the normal responses in fear-based situations.

Afterwards, an opportunity came up for Honnold to have his brain examined by cognitive neuroscientist, Jane Joseph. She put Honnold in an MRI machine and showed him a series of two hundred disturbing images to examine the response of his

---

[10] MacKinnon, J. B. "The Strange Brain of the World's Greatest Solo Climber." *Nautilus*, June 28, 2018. Accessed November 13, 2018. http://nautil.us/issue/61/coordinates/

the-strange-brain-of-the-worlds-greatest-solo-climber-rp.

amygdala. Before the test she said, "I'm excited to see what his brain looks like...check what his amygdala is doing, to see: Does he really have no fear?"

The MRI scan showed that while Honnold had a perfectly healthy amygdala, it did not fire like other test subjects who viewed the same images. In fact, Honnold's amygdala showed no measurable response at all.

Joseph LeDoux, a New York University neuroscientist that has been studying the amygdala's reaction to threats for over 30 years, reports that he has never seen a brain with an undamaged amygdala (like Honnold's) that showed zero activation. LeDoux explained Honnold's unusual results by saying, "His brain is probably predisposed to be less reactive to threats than other people would be naturally responsive to, *simply because of the choices he's made.* On top of that, *these self-imposed strategies that he's using make that even better, or stronger.*"

Jane Joseph, who conducted the test on Honnold's brain, agreed. She concluded, "He's having no internal reactions to these stimuli, but it could be the case that he has such a well-honed regulatory system that he can say, 'OK, I'm feeling all this stuff, my amygdala is going off,' but his frontal cortex is just so powerful that it can calm him down."

What does all this mean? It means that in order to be successful at free soloing, Alex Honnold has learned to control the most primitive parts of his brain, and thereby, control his fear response. Perhaps he described it best of all, "With free-soloing, obviously I know that I'm in danger, but feeling fearful while I'm up there is not helping me in any way."

Honnold is directing his conscious brain to supersede the amygdala's response to serve him better and get the results he wants.

THAT WHICH WE PERSIST IN DOING

It isn't that Alex Honnold doesn't have fear, it's that he has practiced having it over and over again.

When Alex was 19, he attempted his first free solo climb at Corrugation Corner, near Lake Tahoe. Climbs are categorized by difficulty level. Corrugation Corner is a 5.7. To give you some idea of what this means, the Corrugation Corner climb was 15 points easier than Honnold's maximum skill level at that time. But this was the first time he was climbing without a rope and the route is 300 feet high. Honnold remembers knowing that if he fell, he'd die.

Even at the relatively low skill level of 5.7, Honnold ended up really scared that day on Corrugation Corner and overgripped the climb. But despite his fear, he didn't give up. J.B. MacKinnon describes Alex's process, "Honnold donned what he called 'mental armor' and crossed the threshold of fear again and again."

Alex practiced facing his fear repeatedly. Honnold estimates that for every hard pitch he's ever soloed, he's soloed at least 100 easy pitches to practice feeling and knowing his fear intimately. One climb at a time, the impossible began not to be.

Honnold has been free soloing for more than 14 years and in that time he has had his share of terrifying moments—a torn shoe, broken holds, slipped feet, finding himself off-route, being surprised by an animal or bird, or even, as he describes it, "that fraying at the edges, you know, where you've just been up in the void too long." But the key to Honnold's success and his survival was in the familiarity he developed with his fear. As MacKinnon says, "Because he managed to deal with these problems, he gradually dampened his anxieties about them."

The point is not to just sit back in amazement watching Alex Honnold conquer his fear, though amazement is surely warranted. For those of us who are working through our own anxieties and misgivings about our qualification or our ability, there are lessons here for the taking.

The first of these, of course, is practice. It's possible for each of us to get a little better at honnolding—in climbing circles, Alex's name has become a verb—by looking straight into the abyss and facing our fears. MacKinnon concluded, "You may not...be able to quench your amygdala on command, but with conscious effort and gradual, repeated exposure to what you fear, any one of us might muster courage that we didn't know we had."

For most of us, climbing El Capitan ropeless is not one of our big fears because it's not even on our radar. But we each have our own fears and trepidation in our work and our daily interactions that can be overcome or minimized through repeated exposure and practice.

I have a nephew who loves to play the violin, so much so that he wanted to be a concert violinist and study violin performance in college. But no matter how well he practiced his concerto or his sonata, his nerves would get the best of him when it was time to perform. He read somewhere that eating bananas would help calm you by giving you a shot of potassium before a performance. He decided to start eating bananas whenever he had an important audition, recital, or concert.

Trouble was, he hated bananas. He would gag and choke and his eyes would water as he tried to hork down a bunch of bananas. One time, he got so sick he starting vomiting bananas two minutes before he was supposed to take the stage. Let's just say it wasn't his best performance.

His teacher, on hearing of his banana-torture regimen, suggested that he just needed more experience and exposure to performance. Whenever he had a big concert or audition coming, she would require him to perform his piece for 15 people who were not in his family. She required him to do a performance for his orchestra class, a neighbor, his buddies from school, his Sunday School class. One time, he went door-to-door in his neighborhood, asking if he could play Wieniawski's violin concerto for them.

The same principles apply to you, no matter what your work is. Locate and identify your fear and then expose yourself to the threat over and over again. Make 100 cold calls a day, speak in five public places a month, write a blog or record a podcast every week and publish it, volunteer to be the project leader, implement a new marketing strategy every quarter, commit to a monthly digital marketing budget, launch your small business. Whatever action gives you that moment of pause and causes the panic to rise, is the one you should pursue purposefully and regularly.

PRESENT TENSE

Fear is either past-preoccupied or future-focused. It is never part of the present. In the present moment, you are always perfectly fine, alive and well. Fear creeps in when we examine what has happened or what might happen. The most important thing to notice about this universal characteristic of fear is that because it is either a mental creation of something that has already occurred or a mental leap to something that only has a possibility of occurring, *it is not real.* Or rather, *there is no actual threat*—only the thought of one.

Always keep in mind that in the present moment the threat itself is always a projection, simply a mental construct. You can choose to entertain it but you don't have to. It is always a choice.

It should be noted that this is a choice that requires mental discipline. It is easy to let your mind run away with the disaster scenarios ahead of you or relive the moments of catastrophe behind you. This mental time traveling can paralyze you if you're not carefully managing your fear.

For example, Alex Honnold describes how he stays present in moments of alarm, when he's a thousand feet up. He said, "If something happens then you get that spike of fear or that spike of adrenalin, and then sometimes I can find it somewhat hard to recover from something like that. If a foot slips or even if you just suddenly realize you're botching the sequence or something, you might get that jolt of fear...and then sometimes it's hard to recover from that. You have to be disciplined with some deep breaths and think, 'That is now behind me and I am moving forward.' But I haven't experienced that much anymore and I think that's partially because that's something you build up to."

Notice how Honnold acknowledges that he has to recover from those moments of fear. He does this through mental discipline—taking deep breaths, coming back to the present where everything is fine, and forcing the threat to stay behind him in the past where it belongs.

At one point, I was working towards a new product launch. The development ended up taking far longer than I wanted and there were lots of bugs to figure out to make sure the product would deliver on its promises. I had a few of those moments like Alex Honnold, when the original launch date came and went, and that jolt of fear went through me, thinking of the investors, all our work and effort to prepare, the delayed earnings projections, and a thousand other anxieties.

Over and over, I forced my mind back to where I was in the present—not preoccupied with the past and how this could have been avoided, not jumping ahead to crash-and-burn scenarios in which I would have to file bankruptcy or disappoint my investors. I just worked a day at a time on what needed to be done right then. Just like Honnold, I would remind myself that "That is now behind me and I am moving forward." In the present, everything was always fine. In the present, I was still alive and well. In the present, we were still working towards our goal, overcoming one setback at a time. Feeling fearful was not going to help me in any way.

BABY STEPS

If I thought it would help, I would tell you to go ahead and be scared. I'd tell you to do all the worrying and fretting and agonizing you wanted. But worry and fear just pretend to be necessary. These are lies. Worry and fear are never necessary and they are certainly never useful.

I've never free soloed anything, but I understand the discipline required to not let your mind run away in fear. I am the mother of four children, each of whom I brought into this world through childbirth, without medical intervention or any kind of pain medication.

I found that it was easy, in the thick of a prolonged, searing contraction or when there was very little space between contractions, to become overwhelmed and frightened. Your mind wants to panic, recalling the pain you've already been through, and moving ahead to imagine how much more you still have to endure. This is the big unknown variable in any labor: How long? If you slip into the past or get spooked about the future, you can easily find yourself in the grip of pure, unadulterated fear that quickly spirals out of control.

When you are in the middle of labor, deep breathing techniques are often encouraged and turn out to be surprisingly useful. From experience, I think this is less about pain management and more about mind management than anything else. It centers you fully in the present.

If you can breathe and stay present, disciplining your mind to ignore what has already happened and not fast forward to possible disasters ahead, the fear loses its power. Quieting my mind through each contraction, I focused on the present, the immediate now, this one contraction, this one moment of incredible pressure in which I was very uncomfortable, certainly, but in which I was also not in any real danger.

When your amygdala receives and processes a threat, it automates a flight or fight response to remove you from the threatening situation. It's there to preserve and protect you. However, in most situations—like Honnold on the face of El Capitan or me breathing through contractions—neither fight nor flight is going to help. In fact, either will make things considerably worse.

It is no different as you face whatever fears are keeping you from accomplishing the things you want. Flight is putting distance between you and your dreams. Fight is not allowing you to see the things you need to learn to move toward your goal in meaningful ways. Whether you need to present a vital capital project to the board or pass your boards to get your medical license, untamed fear won't help you accomplish your goals.

For example, let's imagine you've always wanted to write a book. Whenever you attempt to begin, fear sidles up and starts feeding you reasons to panic. It starts in the past: *you've never written a book so how do you know you can, you've started Chapter One a hundred times and it's still terrible, your ninth grade English teacher said you were the worst writer he had ever seen, you have big dreams but you never really accomplish anything.*

If that's not enough to initiate the flight response, it moves on to the future: *what if nobody reads it, what if you look stupid, what if people are offended, what if you never finish, what if you finish but no one wants to publish it, what if you find out you have nothing to say, what if you fail again.*

By now, you've likely fled back into the cave where your amygdala senses that you are once again safe and sound. Except that you have not made any progress toward scaling your "El Capitan."

If instead, you quiet your mind to focus on the present, you are much more likely to write Chapter One. You simply ignore your screaming amygdala and recognize that everything is fine. You are just sitting at your desk, typing on a keyboard. There is no danger here. Exercising your Honnold-like discipline, purposefully disregard all the brain's evidence from the past and the panic-inducing anxiety about the future. Every time the brain offers another flight option, remind yourself, "It doesn't matter. I'm just writing this one chapter today. I'm just putting 1500 words on the page." You stay present, with this paragraph, with this sentence, and move word by word towards your goal.

Slowing things down and isolating your actual threats to only the very present moment—where you are never in any real danger—will allow you to move towards those big, audacious goals without systemic panic taking over. Manage your mind and you'll manage your fear.

TRUST ME, I'M A DOCTOR

For most of us, our fears are varied and many. We have addressed many of them in more detail throughout other chapters in this book, and each of us has a quiver full of even more. The truth is, you are never going to get your hands around all of them, successfully removing them one at a time until you can walk around fearless and confident in every aspect of your life.

The problem is not that we have so many fears. The problem is that we let them dictate all our results (or lack of them). Many of us are waiting around to feel confident or find evidence that we can now be confident in our abilities before we proceed towards our goals. However, this is not how it works.

If you are waiting for a reason to feel confident, you will wait forever. Confidence, like any other feeling, including fear, is created with our thoughts, not our actions. The thought always comes first. This means that if we choose thoughts that produce fear (a feeling), we cannot simultaneously be thinking thoughts that produce confidence (also a feeling). Instead, you get stuck in a thought loop that never arrives at confidence no matter what the outside evidence suggests.

Both Alex Honnold, ascending the face of El Capitan, and me, descending into the throes of deep labor, need to be thinking the thoughts that generate confidence in order to have a chance of being successful. Neither of us can wait until we accomplish the challenge in order to get the confidence to reach our goal. We need that confidence all along the way to allow us to overcome our obstacles. What good will it do us after its all over?

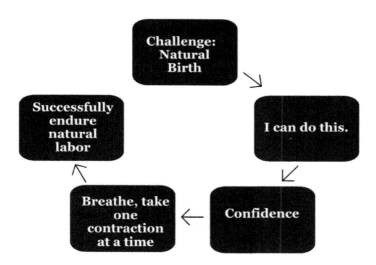

Confidence, then, is not dependent on end results. We need to create the feeling of confidence *first* in order to act and get the results. This is a huge distinction.

Can you see that if you try to do it backwards, needing the evidence of your qualification first, you get stuck? You never get to a place where you can act with confidence or certainty, and then panic is quick to follow. This is another reason why so many of us are not accomplishing our dreams.

Hugh Laurie, probably most famous for his acting role on the TV series *House*, also plays piano in a blues band, sings, and is as comfortable on the stage as he is in front of the camera. He jumps from passion to passion depending on what is really exciting him at the time. Some time ago he gave an interview in which he said, "It's a terrible thing in life to wait until you're ready. I have this feeling now that actually no one is ever ready to do anything. There is almost no such thing as ready. There is only now."

Laurie isn't talking about not being prepared. His skills are always honed and he's always improving them. What he's elucidating is the idea that no matter your skill level, you may never feel fully "ready" (or confident) to do a thing. And again, if you are waiting until that feeling magically descends upon you, it's never going to happen. As he says, "There is almost no such thing as ready."

For Laurie, for Honnold, for me, for you—no matter our level of preparation—there is never going to be a moment of complete "readiness." Our minds are in a thought contest of sorts, in which we beat back the thoughts producing fear and replace them with thoughts producing confidence. Over and over again. And from there we act. The mental management and discipline will then have to continue all through the process, until we reach our goals. It is ongoing. It is constant. There is no confident, "I'm perfectly ready" finish line out there.

THE ROAD LESS TRAVELED

Do you remember that game you used to play on long car trips with your family? It's a memory game, where you say, "I'm going on a trip and I'm taking apples." And then the next person says, "I'm going on a trip and I'm taking boots and apples." And on and on you go, each person using the next letter in the alphabet and adding items that you're taking on your imaginary trip. The goal is to remember the entire list. If you forget one of the items, you're out and it's the next person's turn to try.

When it comes to reaching our goals, I think it can be very helpful to use this little phrase with fear. "I'm writing a book and I'm taking fear" or "I'm starting my own business and I'm taking fear" or "I'm hiking the Grand Canyon this year and I'm taking fear."

I first learned this concept from Elizabeth Gilbert in her book, *Big Magic,* and I've used the principle in lots of different situations. I find that it works every time.

The idea is that fear is always going to be there. For those of us with a functioning amygdala, it's a normal, natural part of everyday existence. No matter how many babies you have or how many 1000-foot rock faces you scale, at some point fear is going to show up. It's part of the deal. It is your constant and predictable travel companion on the road to any and every goal you want to achieve.

Rather than spending all your energy resisting it when it shows up with its extra luggage and its suggested list of annoying detours, you can just recognize that it's a necessary part of your human experience, especially when you are taking your life to a new level. Going somewhere? Fear's going too.

But—and this is the important part—fear never gets to drive.

Fear never gets to hold the steering wheel. It doesn't get to give directions, question the route, consult the map, or even control the radio. It just gets to sit in the back with its headphones on and go for a ride, hitching a lift with you on the way to your dreams.

Now you might argue that it's taking up valuable space in your car and you hate looking at it every time you glance in the rearview mirror. All of that is true. But I find that if I spend all my time and energy trying to get fear out of the car, I never get out of the driveway. It's so much better to drop the resistance, let fear bum a ride, and begin your journey toward your goals. Imagine how surprised fear will be when you get out of the car at your intended destination.

And when you set off on your next goal, don't be surprised when fear shows up for another ride. "Hello again. I'm going on a trip and I'm taking fear." Over time, you two are going to log some serious miles together and arrive at some incredible destinations. El Capitan, here we come!

EXERCISES TO MANAGE FEAR

1. Name the Fear

    In this exercise, you will identify the fear that is holding you back from your goal and see how you are manifesting the exact threat you are trying to avoid.

    Think of your goal. This can be a daily goal, a weekly goal, a yearly goal. (It can be helpful to run this exercise for goals of all sizes and time frames.)

    What is your fear?

    When you think this fearful thought, what action (or inaction) do you take?

    What result does that action give you?

    Notice how your result proves your original fearful thought. Isn't that fascinating? Notice how amazing your brain is and how ridiculous the fear is.

2. Take Action Regardless

    Use the combined techniques of staying present and "I'm going to _____, and I'm taking fear."

    Determine a daily, specific action you want to take towards your goal. For 30 consecutive days, perform the action. When fear shows up, don't be surprised. It's going with you. Acknowledge that it's allowed to come, but you are driving.

    Every time fear wants to pipe up and offer suggestions about turning around or giving up, just stay in the present moment.

Complete your action for that one day. The next day do it again. Make friends with fear along the way. After 30 days, look at how much you accomplished even though fear went with you.

After Magno passed all his nursing prerequisites at the community college, he applied to a few nursing schools, but was not accepted. The nursing programs were competitive and though he had received acceptance into the colleges and universities themselves, he did not get into any of the nursing programs.

One day he got a phone call that some of the prospective students had dropped out of the program and he was next on the list. Did he still want in?

Magno said he had never wanted anything more. He started the next week.

Nursing school was difficult. He managed to pass the first semester—it was a struggle, but he passed—but then decided he could no longer work at Costco and go to nursing school. It was too hard to manage his course load with his work schedule. He got a job as a CNA at a local hospital while he went to nursing school.

After three years, Magno finished nursing school, but he still had to pass the exam to begin practicing as a nurse. NCLEX is a national exam for nursing licensure. It is a very intimidating test with over 240 questions. The test either ends after you pass a specific number of questions and you get your license, or it shuts down if you answer too many questions incorrectly. If the test stops because enough questions are not answered correctly, you have to wait three months to take the test again.

Magno said, "The first time I took the test, I think I got through almost all of the test, almost all the questions, when the test shut down. I flunked."

When Magno returned three months later to take the test the second time, halfway through the test, it closed down. The test is timed and applicants are given three hours to complete it. Magno had run out the clock. In his effort to work slowly and *accurately in order to pass, he had inadvertently gone over the time limit. If you don't finish the test in the allotted three hours, you fail.*

Magno had to take the NCLEX exam a third time. He had now been studying and trying for nine months, but on the third try, he passed.

Magno had a philosophy that "If you can do it, I can do it." It extended to anything he wanted to learn as well: "If you can know it, I can know it." But that did not mean that he could do it or know it the first time he did it.

In fact, there were many moments of failure along the way. Because of his limitations with the English language and given his rigorous medical classes, he failed more than one class. But he never let it mean that he couldn't do it. It only meant he couldn't do it yet. He didn't spend any time wallowing in shame or self-pity or despair. He didn't tell himself it was impossible. He told himself the truth—that he could do whatever he wanted as long as he never gave up.

In Magno's mind, he was either succeeding or he was learning. It didn't matter how long it took or how many tries it took, Magno never saw it as failure. It was simply another step along the way.

CHAPTER 8

FAILURE

"Failure is simply an opportunity to begin again, this time more intelligently."

-Henry Ford

When comedian Mike Birbiglia was first working on his new comedy show about parenthood, he happened to be performing at a college trying out the new jokes. The material completely bombed. Recalling the experience, he laughed, "As I thought about it after, I realized that not only did this audience not *have* kids, they didn't even *know* anybody who had kids." It was a subject completely outside his audience's consciousness. They couldn't relate. The material was not funny to them. They didn't get it.

Birbiglia then called his agent and counterintuitively said, "Hey, I'm working on this new material. Just book me at a ton of colleges." Instead of trying to find the right audience for his material, Birbiglia decided that if he could figure out how to make this subject funny to college students, then he would really have something—he'd have comedy gold. He was pursuing failure in order to learn exactly what would make the show a success.

To accept failure as part of your journey is one thing, but to pursue a course that will almost guarantee it, like Birbiglia did, is another one altogether. Particularly when we feel unqualified for the work we are doing, this goes against every instinct we have.

IT'S NATURAL

The fear of failure is really just a fear of exposure and embarrassment. It's scary because it just feels so *public*. While you may have spent years feeling unqualified, this has primarily been an internal struggle. When we fail, however, our inadequacies or insufficiencies are now on full display for the whole world to see. There is now actual evidence that we are lacking—confirming our long-held suspicions—and the fear of this terrible vulnerability is almost insurmountable.

We are biologically programmed to conform to the group. Experiencing a failure is a terrifying way to stand out from everybody else. We've separated ourselves from the herd. It's like a flashing neon light for every predator out there: Weak Animal! Eat him first!

As illogical as this concern may seem in a world without a lot of man-eating predators around, our brains are hard-wired to reward us for "staying with the group." Being like everyone else feels safe and comforting because our brains give us a little hit of oxytocin to reinforce that behavior. Failure on the other hand, is a form of isolation that feels vulnerable and alarming on a very deep level.

It's critical to remember that if our goal is to evolve and grow and push ourselves, we have to ignore the brain's reinforcements of biologically-safe behaviors and step outside our comfort zone. The old programming is no longer serving us, particularly if we have dreams and aspirations to live our lives at a higher level.

In addition to our biological programming, when we dare to fail, we have to overcome our social programming as well. *How dare*

116

you leave the herd? How dare you leave the cave? Who do you think you are? Do you think you're special? It turns out that the fear of failure is just the fear of shame in disguise: shame for who we are and shame for who we aren't; shame for what we don't know and shame for what we may have learned the hard way; shame for what we want and shame for what we don't; shame for daring to succeed and shame for failing instead; shame for trying and shame for even thinking about trying.

The real problem with all this shame is that shame likes to hide and stay out of sight. Unfortunately, in the case of failure, this is exactly the opposite of what needs to happen. In order to use failure purposely to create our success, like Birbiglia did, it requires an open, thorough, and frank examination of each and every failure. The more data the better.

GAME TAPE

In October 2009, there was a conference held in San Francisco that was the first of its kind. It was a one-day conference on failure. Cassandra Phillipps founded FailCon to celebrate the failures in the tech community of Silicon Valley and to provide a venue to learn from them. Phillipps felt that the shame that generally surrounded a business or startup failure prevented the careful examination and subsequent learning that could be of benefit in future ventures.

This is a common practice in athletic losses. Rather than ignoring or glossing over a loss or a failure, athletes and their coaches rewind the tape over and over again to discover exactly where they could have executed their game plan better. They use the negative outcomes as a way to glean more information and make them better in their next game.

Payton Manning famously studied hours and hours of game tape in order to be prepared for his opponents. But even more noteworthy, when he became the starting quarterback of his college football team, he requested that the practices be filmed as well. Not only did he take the opportunity to learn from mistakes during the games, he wanted to learn from the failures and experiences of practice as well.

Our willingness to look at and learn from our failures with curiosity rather than shame or embarrassment is a key element of becoming an unqualified success. Manning, Birbiglia, and others like them are willing to examine and reexamine their missteps for the sake of marked improvement.

Too many times, people who feel unqualified in any area are fearful or hesitant to look too closely at a failure because then they will be forced to come face-to-face with their inadequacies. However, this tactic only ensures that the weakness cannot be identified and then addressed and strengthened. As Abraham Lincoln pointed out, "Men are greedy to publish the success of their efforts, but meanly shy as to publishing the failures of men. Men are ruined by this one-sided practice of concealment of blunders and failures."

When Sara Blakely, a self-made billionaire and the founder of Spanx, was growing up, her father asked her one question every day at the dinner table: "What have you failed at today?" She reports that her father was disappointed if she and her brother didn't have an example to share and she felt some pressure to fail. This airing of failures around the kitchen table, allowed Blakely to look at failure wholly differently—as something to be sought rather than avoided.

WHAT'S IN A WORD

One of the challenges when it comes to talking about failure is that the word itself fails us. The original term was created in the 19th century to describe the economic event of bankruptcy, when there was simply no more money to continue the venture. It wasn't until much later that it was applied to other endeavors and it acquired an emotional connotation.

But, like the word success, it means different things to different people and it lets us down by being unable to characterize the true nature of failure. As it is, the word implies an end, a finality. However, when we progress from one failure to another, viewing each unsuccessful experience as its own starting place along the road to our goal, failure is a woefully inadequate descriptor.

It is not the end. It is only more information, more data, to let you progress more intelligently forward. Show after show, Mike Birbiglia was acquiring as much data as possible—one failed joke after another, one line that didn't land at a time: This works. That doesn't. What if I did it like this instead?

On the journey toward the goal, where exactly is the line between failure and success, where does one begin and one end? Wasn't the former intrinsically, inseparably connected to the later? If that's true, couldn't you rightfully label all of it success? The failures are just the way to get there.

HEARTBREAKING FAILURES

During the early, pioneering days of open-heart surgery, there were more than a few failures. When Dr. Russell M. Nelson was in medical school in the late 1940s, he was taught that no doctor should ever touch a human heart. At this time, it was widely believed that if a beating heart was touched, it would throw the heart out of rhythm and trigger a heart attack.

Through study and research, Dr. Nelson and his colleagues created the first artificial heart-lung machine, which could take over a patient's circulation, theoretically allowing the doctors to perform surgery on an unbeating heart. They tried it first successfully on a dog, using the artificial heart-lung machine to circulate the dog's blood while they operated directly on the dog's heart.

They postulated that the same operation could be done on a human heart, allowing them to access the heart and perform repairs never before imagined or attempted. During this time, Dr. Nelson was asked to operate on a little girl who had congenital heart disease. The family had already lost her older brother to the disease. They brought this second child to Dr. Nelson, hoping for healing through the revolutionary new surgery.

For a number of reasons, Dr. Nelson was not optimistic about a positive outcome from the surgery, but eventually relented to the pleadings of the girl's parents and agreed to do everything he could to try to save her life. Dr. Nelson wrote, "Despite my best efforts, the child died."

Later, these same parents brought another daughter to him when she was only 16 months old, who had also been born with a malformed heart, the same condition that affected her siblings. Dr. Nelson again performed an operation at the family's request, but this third, precious child also died.

Dr. Nelson recorded, "This third heartbreaking loss in one family literally undid me. I went home grief stricken. I threw myself upon our living room floor and cried all night long.

The failure was almost more than he could bear. His wife, Dantzel, stayed by his side all night, listening as he repeatedly declared, "I'm through. I'll never do another heart operation as long as I live." Around 5:00 the next morning, Dantzel lovingly asked, "Are you finished crying? Then get dressed. Go back to the lab. Go to work! You need to learn more. If you quit now, others will have to painfully learn what you already know."[11]

---

[11] Nelson, Russell M. *From Heart to Heart*. N.p.: Quality Press, 1979.

These early failures in open-heart surgery were the only path to the success Dr. Nelson knew was eventually possible in his field. Whether they were made by him or someone else, they were the exclusive way to the medical answers the world needed.

CULTURE OF FAILURE

Failure is simply the natural result of innovation and creativity as we push past our current boundaries and explore what's still possible. They cannot be separated. Reframing failure as the way to the goal, rather than an unpleasant detour or the end of the road, can change everything.

At the Mayo Clinic, for example, in an effort to diminish the embarrassment and shame that can accompany these important, requisite failures, they instituted something called the Queasy Eagle Award. The award was given out for the ideas that, despite significant effort and inspiration, didn't quite make it.

The results speak for themselves. Before the Queasy Eagle Award, the organization had very few ideas for patents, but 18 months after creating the award, they had 245 ideas submitted, many of which merited new patents. Encouraging the examination of failures, rather than condemning them, made an incredible difference in the innovation of the entire organization.

Other companies like Google and Gore have discovered the power of this same philosophy. Intuit, the accounting software giant, also gives a special award for "Best Failure" and regularly holds "failure parties." Co-founder Scott Cook explains, "At Intuit we celebrate failure because every failure teaches something important that can be the seed for the next great idea."

REACHING YOUR GOOOOOAAAAAALLLLLLLLLL!

Brazil's national soccer team is almost universally recognizable in their green and yellow uniforms. But the team did not always dress this way. In the 1950 World Cup tournament, the team wore white and were the host team for the rest of the world. They were the clear favorites of the tournament and expected to win handily that year, so much so that there were victory celebrations even before the final match was played. It was all but done.

However, in a stunning upset, Uruguay went on to win the final match 2-1, leaving the entire country devastated. In grief, they permanently changed their uniform colors and didn't play in the new Maracanazo stadium for four years.

Aldo Rebelo, the Brazilian minister of sport, said of the national tragedy, "Losing to Uruguay in 1950 not only impacted Brazilian football. It impacted the country's self-esteem."[12] Others claimed the loss effectively paralyzed the country, emotionally and psychologically.

Moacir Barbosa, the goalkeeper of the Brazilian team, suffered the most as a result of the tragic defeat. As goalkeeper, he became the one responsible for the defeat. After allowing the two opposing goals, he alone shouldered the blame and suffered endless criticism from his countrymen. Shortly before his death Barbosa expressed his pain, "Under Brazilian law, the maximum sentence is 30 years. But my imprisonment has been for 50 years."

---

[12] Schorr, Matthew. "The Maracanazo: Brazilian Tragedy and the 1950 World Cup." Soccer Politics Blog. Last modified 2013. Accessed February 25, 2019. https://sites.duke.edu/wcwp/tournament-guides/world-cup-2014/world-cup-2014-fan-guide/anglophone-version/the-1950-world-cup-brazilian-tragedy/.

Now the mistakes I make in our business or as a leader in our company haven't yet ruined the self-esteem of an entire nation or put anyone's life at risk, but they can feel just as devastating when they cost us time or money or make someone else's job harder.

For each of us, failure is an unavoidable part of our work. But given too much power, these errors can have the same effect as Brazil's 1950 World Cup loss, psychologically paralyzing us and diminishing our abilities to continue forward toward our goals.

So how do we move on after a misstep or failure? How do we turn our errors, however big or small, into learning opportunities rather than stumbling blocks to future progress? In addition to reframing our view of failure as the path to achievement, there are a couple more things to keep in mind to overcome the mental obstacles after a perceived failure.

THEM'S THE FACTS

As we evaluate our mistakes or failures, it's easy to exaggerate the damage and spin out emotionally, letting shame take center stage and control the narrative. Eliminate the shame, regret, and guilt by sifting out the facts. What are the actual losses? Determine what part is actual circumstance and what part is just the story you are telling yourself about it. Turn it into math.

For example, in our business, we ramp up our workforce during the Arizona monsoon season. We expect and anticipate that we will need more technicians to meet the needs caused by the severe winds, heavy rains, and flooding that affect our valley every summer. Of course, we don't control the weather. Some seasons are worse than others. There have been years where the extra manpower wasn't completely necessary and appeared to be a bad business decision.

I can let those decisions paralyze me the next time monsoon season rolls around, or I can separate out the facts: this season we hired x amount of people or we paid x amount more than we needed to in salaries. These are just numbers. Taking the emotion out of the equation allows you to neutralize the situation and get some of your power back.

This does not mean that you don't review the game tape. You do. That is a critical part in designing and creating the success you are seeking. But you don't disparage yourself or your abilities in the process. When Tom Brady or Payton Manning are analyzing game tape, they are doing so to get more data, to do it better the next time, to figure out why something didn't work, not to find ammunition to destroy their confidence and fuel their insecurities.

Use the facts to analyze where you need to put in the work or do things differently. But do it with a neutral, curious eye. Don't create unproductive stories and thought loops that increase shame. These will not propel you forward but leave you lost and stuck.

When Birbiglia is trying to find the best comedy for his show, for instance, he is asking himself, "I wonder why that line doesn't work? Is there a way to say that differently?" not, "Why did I ever think I could be a comedian? What business do I have being out here on stage? Why even try?"

Once you have the facts separated, recognize that by themselves, the facts are neither good or bad. They just are. It's just information. You get to think whatever you want about those circumstances.

When Alan Mulally was the CEO at Ford, he used to tell his leaders and employees, "The situation is not good or bad. The situation is just the way it is. We get to decide what to do about it." With this thought, Mulally led Ford to one of the greatest turnarounds in business history.

IT'S THE THOUGHT THAT COUNTS

The biggest determining factor in your ability to use your failures to generate success is your own thoughts. *What we make the failure mean is what counts.* If we make it mean that something didn't work, then we can analyze it and move forward. If we make it mean that we can't make it work, then we are in trouble.

Thinking about failure as the means to success rather than an indictment of our own qualifications or abilities takes the sting out, removes the shame, and allows room for helpful, insightful questions that get us closer to the goal. It is this honest curiosity that makes room for the innovation and discovery that results in eventual success.

Some high achievers take this idea even further: not just accepting or curiously tolerating failure but actively seeking it. As IBM's CEO Thomas Watson Sr. once said, "The fastest way to succeed is to double your failure rate." Financial advisor and author, Ramit Sethi even recommends keeping a file of failures with a specific monthly goal to fill the file. For example, his goal is to achieve five serious failures every month to add to his file.

Accepting or even seeking failure as a way to achieve success is a completely new way of thinking. Traditionally, our brains see failure as a valid reason to give up completely, to hide in shame, and to quit. This is a gross overreaction created by our brain's inherent desires to both conserve energy and remain unnoticed within the herd.

But again, this kind of thinking will not serve us as we strive to reach our goals.

It can be much more useful to think of our efforts not in black-and-white terms of either failure or success, but instead in terms of accomplishment that is generally "trending upward." This idea is that we all have a starting place, whether it's in our business or in our personal lives, and then we have the place that we want to get to:

As we start to work on our goals, there are inevitable failures and setbacks. As we've already discussed, these are simply part of the process. However, in an attempt to protect us, our brain will overreact and tell us things like: "See, I knew it was impossible to change" or "We're never going to get there" or even, "Why did we think we could do this? We should give up now."

This is where the way we think about failure becomes so critical.

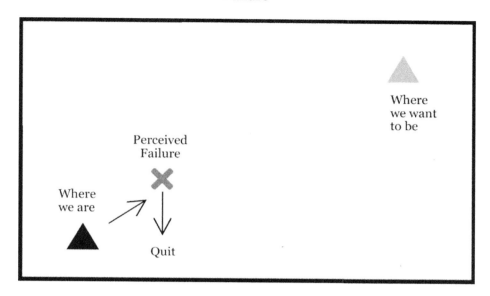

If we control the narrative in our minds, purposely choosing our thoughts about the "failure" by refusing to make it mean anything about us and our abilities or qualifications and only view it as a source of additional information about the process or path to our goal, then we can continue moving forward, trending upward toward our goal.

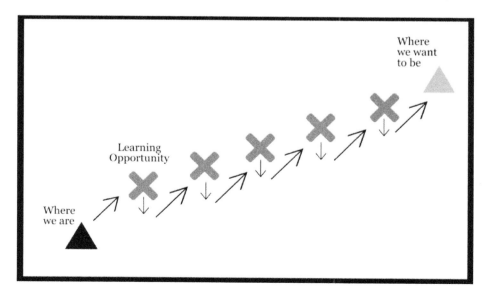

Over time, you can see the trend upward, closing the gap between where we are now and where we want to be, despite the number or severity of any perceived failures along the way. The way you think about each failure will ultimately determine where you end up.

SUCCESS VS. MASTERY

In addition to reframing the meaning of *failure*, it can also be useful to redefine *success* as well. Like failure, the word "success" implies an end, an event, a moment of achievement, and one that necessarily requires an outside opinion or the consensus of others. This leaves those of us seeking success in the unenviable position of chasing an arbitrary definition of worth and validation with a single destination.

If success is an event, mastery, as an alternative, is a journey. Mastery represents a constant pursuit of improvement, progress, and excellence, rather than just arriving at a goal.

Mastery is the constant quest to close the gap from where you are now and where you want to be, which has an ever-shifting horizon. Those who focus on mastery do their work for the reaching, not the arriving. When Duke Ellington was asked which of the 3000 songs he wrote over his lifetime was his favorite, he replied, "Always the next one. Always the one I have yet to compose."

It turns out that we thrive when we still have more to do. This is known as the phenomenon of the "near win." The idea is that a near win will propel you forward with more power and energy than any actual win will. For the ambitious, this is the sweet spot for achievement.

Thomas Gilovich, a psychology professor at Cornell, has done studies on Olympic athletes since the 1992 Barcelona Olympics.

It turns out that bronze medalists are much happier than silver medalists because of the thoughts they each have about "what might have been." For bronze medalists, for example, Gilovich found that it was easy for them to imagine how close they came to not making the podium at all. They were happy to have received a podium placing. On the other hand, for the silver medalists, it was not hard for them to see just how close they were to getting the gold and how little separated them from the *top* of the podium.

Gilovich went on to study the subsequent frustration of silver medalists. He found that they, more than anyone else in the field, even those who won gold, were the most focused on follow-up competitions. The near-win was an incredible factor of motivation.

In 1984, Jackie Joyner-Kersee missed the gold in the heptathlon by only five points. The heptathlon is a long, multi-disciplinary event in which competitors earn thousands of points in order to win, and she was edged out by only five. She was so motivated in the following Olympics that she won the gold in the heptathlon and set a world record that still stands today. In 30 years, no athlete has even come close.

The point is that rather than seeing your near wins as a demoralizing failure, they can be used instead, as powerful motivation for achieving even more. If success isn't reduced to a single event or limited to a specific moment of achievement, the mindset of mastery can serve as potent propulsion for incredible accomplishment.

LEADING BY EXAMPLE

Finally, consider how you lead through failure.

It should come as no surprise that as a leader, the way you think and talk about failure has a powerful effect on your company's ability to overcome and ultimately succeed. From coaches and quarterbacks to parents and mentors to CEOs and entrepreneurs, the single greatest factor in your organization's eventual victory is your ability to curiously process and then learn from failure and adversity.

The late Roberto Goizueta got years of good-natured ribbing from the New Coke fiasco that occurred during his tenure as CEO of Coca-Cola. As Richard Farson and Ralph Keyes pointed out in Harvard Business Review, "Admitting his mistake conveyed to his employees better than a hundred speeches or a thousand memos that 'learning failures,' even on a grand scale, were tolerated."

In another example, former CEO of 3M, L.D. DeSimone, regularly and repeatedly recounted how he had aggressively tried to prevent the development of Thinsulate, which became one of 3M's most successful products. Again, Farson and Keyes wrote, "By being so candid about his near blunder, DeSimone powerfully conveyed that it's okay to be wrong and to admit it when you are."

How you think about failure is the only part of failure that matters. Whether you're the leader of a Fortune 500 company or running your small business from your garage and your laptop, it comes down to that. As you push the boundaries of technology, science, art, or just the limitations of your own brain, you're going to meet a lot of failure and a lot of success along the way.

And if you're doing it right, you probably won't be able to tell them apart.

EXERCISES FOR USING FAILURE TO FUEL SUCCESS

Choose one or more of the following exercises to change the way you think about failure.

1. Exercise 1: What is your biggest failure?

    In one paragraph, write the story of your failure.

    Is there another way to write the story? Rewrite the story of your failure, reaching a different conclusion.

    For example, if your story is that you invested and lost your life savings in an MLM because you're not good at sales and it was the worst thing that ever happened, can you retell it and make it the best thing that ever happened? Remember, your failure is only a thought. What is an alternative thought that can propel you forward?

    Can you retell all your failures into a story of success?

2. Exercise 2: Keep a Record

    For the next month, keep a file of your failures. Try to accrue as many as possible by attempting things that are hard or out of your comfort zone. (Do not accrue any through lack of effort or not showing up.)

    Do this challenge with a friend or colleague. See who can achieve the most failures by the end of the month.

3. Exercise 3: Dream Big

    Write down the one thing you would you do if you knew you could not fail?

Assume that you only fail if you quit. Everything else is simply the path to your goal.

Every week this month, take one action towards that goal.

Magno now had two associate's degrees and a bachelor's degree in nursing with a minor in business administration. He had passed the nursing licensing exam and he was working as a nurse. He was good at his job and did very well in his chosen profession. He became a house supervisor at the hospital and was part of an elite team of 17 other nurses who had a leadership role.

He could have stopped there. Magno held an estimable position and had a great salary. As a house supervisor, he oversaw the nursing operations of the entire hospital.

But Magno knew he could go even further. When he worked at Costco, his coworker was pursuing his degree as a nurse practitioner. Magno had asked him about it. His friend explained that as a nurse practitioner he could diagnose patients and prescribe medication. Nurse practitioners did the same work as doctors. Magno knew that if he got more education, he would have even more opportunities. It was up to him. He could go as far as he wanted.

Magno applied to the University of Utah's master's program to become a nurse practitioner. It was then that he found out that the bachelor's degree program he had attended was accredited nationally. The University of Utah did not accept nationally-accredited nursing degrees into their program, only regionally accredited.

Magno thought his educational journey might be over. But he was still hungry for growth and opportunity so he did more research. He found out that there were master's programs at colleges that accepted nationally accredited bachelor's degrees in Miami, Idaho, and Arizona. Magno started applying.

He applied to two schools in Arizona and was accepted into the nurse practitioner program at Grand Canyon University in Phoenix. But Magno was living in Utah. He still had his job as a nurse and house supervisor and his children were enrolled in school. In order to pursue this new stage of growth he would have to make some big sacrifices. He would have to uproot his family, give up his prominent position and good salary at the hospital, and he would have to go back to school.

Magno was committed to growth. He had begun his journey with a shovel and pair of boots, and he kept growing, job after job, class after class, so that he could evolve and fulfill his purpose and his dreams. Despite the amount of change and discomfort that this next step required, Magno was all in.

Magno said, "I left my dream job. We sold our house. We moved the kids. I was committed."

The story Magno was always telling himself was that he could be more. He could know more. He could do more. He could have more. There was always more—of whatever he wanted. He was always the one in charge of how much more. It was all up to him. "I would ask myself," he said, "How bad do you want it? And then I would do it.

Magno never stopped setting goals or reaching. He was never satisfied that he knew enough or had grown enough. He was hungry for the best possible life—the life he absolutely knew he could have.

CHAPTER 9

HUNGRY FOR GROWTH

"Growth is painful. Change is painful. But, nothing is as painful as staying stuck where you do not belong."

-N. R. Narayana Murthy

Chris Sacca, self-made billionaire and former shark on *Shark Tank*, is famously known for attending meetings he wasn't invited to. When he started in an entry-level job at Google, he made it a point to attend every meeting he could, just to see what he could learn—whether or not he was actually invited was irrelevant. Whenever anyone questioned his presence in the meeting he would simply say, "Oh, I'm just here to take notes."

Sacca attended so many meetings he became a sort of fixture, so that people came to expect him in meetings "far above his paygrade." In this way, he was able to learn from the founders and leaders of the company and make huge strides in his personal business development and understanding. He went on to become a leader in the company and then founded his own venture capital fund, Lowercase Capital, which invested in early-stage technology companies like Twitter, Instagram, Uber, and Kickstarter. In 2017, he was number two on Forbes' Midas List of Top Tech Investors.

What Sacca understood early on is that in order to achieve his potential he needed more information. He was willing to put himself in situations where he was the least qualified person in the room in order to get that information. If you are willing to acknowledge what you don't know and then stop at nothing to find the answers, there might not be a more powerful combination to achieving what you want.

WHY CAN'T WE JUST BE?

Before we talk about how to create a mindset and a lifestyle that is hungry for growth and continual learning, it's important to first consider *why* we want to operate like this.

A couple of years ago my sister was talking at the dinner table about something new she had learned while listening to her favorite podcast. She was talking animatedly and excitedly about her insights and new goals and encouraging her children to adopt some of her new strategies. Her then 17-year-old daughter sighed, clearly exasperated, and asked her, "Why do we always have to improve? Why can't we just *be*?"

I've thought a lot about that question after my sister related the story to me. And I think it bears examining.

Underneath my niece's question, of course, is the concern that she isn't enough just as she is. With all our well-meaning talk of self-improvement and growth, there can be a demoralizing, underlying assumption that we need fixing.

Not only is this assumption categorically wrong, it is a powerless position from which to begin. Continuous improvement and growth are always optional and are never indications or statements of our worth or value.

One of the biggest fallacies that we can buy into when we feel unqualified is the idea that if we improve and change and grow then we can outrun or eliminate our feelings of lack, the thought being that if we know more and evolve more, then we will finally be worthy.

This erroneous thinking is problematic for a few reasons. The first is that, as we've already established, our feelings are not changed by our circumstances or, in this case, by our improvement. Our feelings are only ever changed by our thoughts. Additionally, we are already 100 percent worthy and valuable. Adding to our accomplishments or our resume doesn't make us better people. It just allows us to use more skills and have more enjoyment as we make our contribution in the world.

When we operate out of a need to improve in order to prove something about ourselves, it induces us to set goals and seek growth and development out of desperation rather than enthusiasm. Chased by our inadequacies, we seek quick growth and immediate results. We aren't growing for growth's sake, we are growing to avoid ourselves. This subtle form of self-loathing creates a painful growth curve and usually lots of self-flagellation along the way.

Finally, when we grow in an attempt to escape ourselves, we will find that the horizon is always moving. When we feel unqualified, the brain likes to find evidence to prove this thought right. Therefore, whatever growth we attempt will never add up sufficiently. The brain moves the marker every time. At no point will we ever arrive at "enough."

Instead, when we operate towards growth and development out of passion, excitement, or enthusiasm, we fuel an internal culture of growth. We seek more learning, personal growth, and goal achievement because it's just more fun to live this way.

COMING UP AGAINST YOURSELF

Another reason why we might want to choose a life of growth and personal development is that it allows you to come up against yourself. It allows you to find the places of personal resistance and fear and learn about yourself as you push forward through discomfort anyway.

After Warren Buffet finished graduate school at Columbia, he returned to Omaha, Nebraska. One day he saw an ad for a Dale Carnegie speaking course. Buffett had a terrible fear of public speaking and panicked anytime the opportunity arose. "I would throw up," he said. "In fact, I arranged my life so that I never had to get up in front of anybody."[13]

But Buffet had big goals, one of which was to become a millionaire by age 35. Warren knew that if he wanted to achieve his lofty goals, he would probably have to do some public speaking. The first time he signed up for the course he dropped it before it started. "I knew I was going to have to speak in public sometimes," Buffett remembered. "The agony was such that just to get rid of the pain I signed up for the course again."

The speaking course was held in a hotel in Omaha and there were about 30 students in the class. Buffett recalls that they were all so terrified they couldn't even say their own names and introduce themselves. They just stood there silently looking at one another.

The students were given a book of speeches and they had to deliver one of them every week. In this low-stakes environment, Buffett learned to get comfortable in front of an audience. Buffett noted the key to learning this new skill: "Some of it is just practice—just doing it and practicing. The way it works is that you learn to get out of yourself."

The way all of it works is learning to get out of yourself. When we push ourselves past our comfort zones to learn things we don't know, our brains offer us all kinds of excuses and

---

[13] Baer, Drake. "Warren Buffett Used To Throw Up Before Public Speaking — Here's How He Mastered It." Business Insider. Last modified December 12, 2014. Accessed December 14, 2018. https://www.businessinsider.com/how-warren-buffett-learned-public-speaking-2014-12.

resistance. But staying in the discomfort, as Buffett did, allows us to get outside of our own heads long enough to see that these are only lies our brain is selling us to keep us safe and small and expending as little energy as possible. Confronting that internal resistance is where real growth occurs.

Anytime we set a goal that brings up negative emotion for us, we can be assured it's a goal worth pursuing. Not just for the achievement of the goal itself—this is actually only a secondary, ancillary benefit—but for what happens to us and how we evolve as we do things in the presence of discomfort.

Like Buffett, I have my own lofty goals. They will undoubtedly involve plenty of public speaking opportunities. So rather than just hope that I will know what to do when the time comes, I hired a speaking coach and took a few classes. I made a purposeful plan to speak publicly three times a month, with or without pay, just for the exposure therapy. I am hungry for growth and going all in. Through the process, there will be lots of practice. But more importantly, there will be plenty of opportunities to see my own brain in action and therefore, many chances to get out of my own way.

Remember that your brain wants to be safe and comfortable much more than it wants you to achieve your goals. One of the most important aspects of continual learning and growth is learning how to get around and overcome this built-in "defense" mechanism. That meta skill will serve you far greater than any goal you ever achieve.

WAYS TO GROW

Once we figure out the powerful reasons behind why we want to grow and stretch ourselves, it's time to get busy doing just that. With that in mind, let's talk about specific ways to go to work when we are hungry for growth in any area of our lives.

First, keep in mind that in order to develop and grow there are two important activities we need to be engaged in: learning and doing. As we just saw with Warren Buffett, in order to grow in the way he wanted, he had to *learn* speaking skills and he had to actually *do the work* and put himself out there in front of people. If you are hungry for growth you will need to do your share of both of them.

I READ SOMEWHERE

Tim Ferriss has made a living asking questions of some of the highest achievers in our society, trying to figure out what makes them different, how they have found success, and what they can teach the rest of us about reaching our goals. One of the things he asks about regularly is the morning routines of these high achievers.

Over the years I have listened to many of Tim's podcasts, and I think one of the most common refrains in the morning routines of his high-achieving guests is the habit they have made of reading every day. They aren't satisfied with their current level of knowledge or understanding—they are always hungry for more.

Mark Cuban, for example, is a voracious reader and estimates reading four to five hours a day. "I read everything I can. I don't care what the source is," Cuban said.[14] He starts with the newspapers and his email inbox. Once current, he moves on to new knowledge acquisition.

Even though Forbes puts Cuban's net worth at nearly $4 billion, Cuban still asserts that continuous learning is the only way to

---

[14] Montag, Ali. "Mark Cuban spends '4 or 5 hours a day' reading — here's what's on his list." CNBC Make It. Last modified September 1, 2018. Accessed January 14, 2019.
https://www.cnbc.com/2018/08/31/what-mark-cuban-reads-every-day.html.

stay competitive. "Particularly in the tech industry, the only constant is change," Cuban explained. "So, you've got to stay up, because otherwise, there is some 12- or 18-year-old kid that is coming in with a better idea to kick your ass."

Cuban's theory is that knowledge gives him an advantage. And it's an advantage he can control, no matter what the other variables in the equation are. Even when he was selling software in Dallas at the beginning of his career, he employed this same advantage by reading programming manuals at night.

"A guy with little computer background could compete with far more experienced guys just because I put in the time to learn all I could," Cuban blogged. "Most people won't put in the time to get a knowledge advantage.

"To this day, I feel like if I put in enough time consuming all the information available, particularly with the net making it so readily available, I can get an advantage in any technology business."

If you don't know, go find out. If they know it, you can know it. There is a world of information out there about any subject you want to know about and getting more knowledge will only make you better at whatever you choose to do. The sources are as varied and readily available as they are numerous.

There is a woman who lives just down the street from me. A few years ago, she started riding motorcycles. Occasionally they wouldn't operate like they were supposed to, so she learned how to fix anything on her bike with the help of YouTube. For Christmas, her kids gave her a "YouTube Certified" patch for her coveralls. She wears it with pride.

If you're hungry for growth, you can learn absolutely anything you want to.

PASSIVE VS. MASSIVE ACTION

Learning is one thing. Doing is another entirely.

I find that when people aren't growing the way they want to it's often because they get stuck "preparing" to act. They get trapped reading or taking another class or studying a little more or just dreaming about their goals. They aren't actually taking any action.

Life-coach Brooke Castillo calls this passive action. As humans, we like taking passive action because it's safe. It makes us feel like we're moving towards our goal without any of the risk. The trouble is passive action can put us in a continuous state of preparation rather than execution.

There comes a point (much sooner than our brains would like us to believe) when passive action needs to take a back seat to actual action. As successful entrepreneur Derek Sivers once told Tim Ferriss, "If all we needed was more information, then everyone would be a billionaire with perfect abs." At some point, you have to act.

This is the critical difference to your personal evolution. Solely consuming information will not produce measurable results in our lives. You must move beyond simple consumption to actual production. Castillo calls this "massive action." Massive action is bold, constructive action that you take and continue to take until you reach your goal—regardless of the obstacles, regardless of the mental resistance, regardless even of your abilities or skills.

Being hungry for growth, remember, must include moments of discomfort and probably a lot of them. Warren Buffett could take a million classes on public speaking (passive action), but until he did the work of giving actual speeches (massive action) he could not gain the skills he needed to overcome his fears and achieve his goals. It is no different for us.

THE DEEP END OF THE POOL

When I was in college I was in a class where I sat next to a boy from Canada. Near the end of the semester he told me about his beginning swimming class. I was from Arizona and so I had been swimming before I could walk. But apparently, where he grew up swimming is not a vital life skill and he had never learned how.

During the course, he had spent class after class putting his face under the water, learning the different strokes, practicing his kicking from the edge of the pool, and repeatedly lifting his arm and turning his head simultaneously to breathe. But on this day, he had to swim for the final exam—he had to jump into the pool, put all his knowledge into action, and swim from one length of the pool to the other. He was terrified. He was sure he was going to drown.

It was one thing to learn about swimming—all the steps and techniques and skills of swimming—but putting it all into action and facing the deep end of the pool by himself was another thing altogether.

When we're hungry to grow, at some point we all have to jump into the pool. We've got to move from observation to action. You can't grow just by learning or thinking about it. You gotta jump.

I have one employee that, in her passion and hunger for growth, has held almost every position in our company. She started in administration and moved to be our water division manager, then to a superintendent position; now she's our controller. I'm certain this isn't the ceiling either. In each position, while she started with some knowledge and understanding, she had no actual experience with the processes and demands of each particular job. She started from scratch. And in every case, she learned and evolved and mastered the job, whatever it was, simply by jumping in.

The distance between passive action and massive action is huge. The thing is, when you're willing to cross it, the difference in your results is just as big.

HOW BAD DO YOU WANT IT?

Growth requires stretching. It is uncomfortable. When we move from passive action to massive action, we are putting ourselves out there. Failure, embarrassment, ridicule, and judgment are now very real possibilities. And, admittedly, it's not for everybody.

Over the past year, in our company we have been working to uplevel the leadership skills of our executive team. We used a matrix to identify "unqualified areas," which allowed us to focus our energy on specific leadership attributes that we wanted to grow and develop.

For some people this kind of stretching and growth is painful enough that they decide they don't want to pursue it. They just aren't hungry for growth in that way. For others, as uncomfortable as the process is, the desire to grow overcomes their reservations and fears and they are able to make significant progress.

It turns out that there is a difference between just wanting something and being truly hungry for it. If you are truly hungry for growth, you will be willing to keep taking massive action despite all the growing pains.

Heather is a member of my executive team who, like many people, doesn't like change. We identified this as the "unqualified area" that Heather wanted to focus on. Restoration is actually an industry full of change—nothing is predictable as we respond to the weather, unforeseen broken pipes, fires, and more. Heather was used to this kind of volatility and unpredictability. But what's even more challenging is the change that happens when an organization scales quickly. Our company went from a $7M company to a $22M company in the space of three years. In order to make that happen, the one thing we do is change.

Even though Heather hates change, she hates staying complacent even more. She was hungry for growth and willing to confront her fears and misgivings, just as Buffett did, in order to reach her goals.

Over the course of three years, we changed everything from our processes to our culture. We redid every procedure and reinvented our business model from square one. Every step in the process required more from our leaders—both in their job requirements and in their belief systems. Each time a new level of adaptation was required, Heather could feel the resistance inside herself. "Sometimes I just felt like this was too much; I can't do that. Then I would ask myself, 'How bad do I want it?' The answer was always, 'Bad enough.'"

All of this work was difficult for Heather to do, but her desire for growth always motivated her to keep taking massive action and do whatever was required.

The CEO of Infusionsoft, Clate Mask, explained that when you're growing as a company, the skills and abilities that got you to $1M won't get you to $3M, and the things that got you to $3M won't get you to $10M. At each level, you have to give up the ideas and processes and procedures that got you there in order to grow to the next place you want to be.

The same is true for us as we try to grow personally or professionally. Whatever got us to this point will not get us to where we want to be. You can't use the same training plan to run a marathon as you used to win a 5K. A different runner is required for a different race.

Often we have firm ideas in our minds about who we are or how we operate. "I'm a follower, but not a leader." "I'm not really an 'ideas' person, but I'm awesome at execution." "I've always done it this way and it's always worked for me." When we are hungry for growth and taking massive action to reach our goals, we often have to give up things and make sacrifices. One of the biggest things we have to give up is our preconceived ideas about ourselves and our abilities. I have found that changing the fundamental way we operate personally and see ourselves is some of the most massive action we will ever do.

BAR NONE

When Lara Merriken was trying to move into manufacturing her now well-known Lärabars, she had to get way out of her comfort zone and learn about things she never needed to know before. She created her first bars in her kitchen with her Cuisinart and a pizza cutter, using the ingredients she purchased in little baggies at a natural-foods grocery store. There was a huge gap between those early days in her own kitchen to having a product on a store shelf, and it involved a very steep learning curve.

Lara said when she started seeing interest in her bars from other people willing to buy them, it was exciting, but she was dismayed at the thought of all she didn't know. She said, "I thought, 'How in the world am I going to manufacture these things? Where am I going to get the ingredients? What do I know about almonds and dates and all that stuff? What do I know about manufacturing equipment?' At the time, I started questioning myself, 'Am I actually going to do this or should I just go to work for Whole Foods? Maybe I'll just do that.'"[15]

---

[15] Raz, Guy. "LARABAR: Lara Merriken." *How I Built This*. Podcast audio. March 18, 2018. Accessed February 25, 2019. https://www.npr.org/2018/06/07/594357259/l-rabar-lara-merriken.

Merriken had a choice; the same choice each of us have: take the easy road or climb the path of growth. If Lara wanted to grow in the way that would allow her to achieve her dream, there was going to be both passive and massive action required, and lots of it.

Lara had to figure out food-grade packaging requirements and trademark considerations, along with manufacturing, selling, and distribution. She also needed a capital investment to produce her original, five-bar product line, which required a business plan and profit forecasting, none of which she knew anything about. Most of all, though, Lara had to give up her own limiting beliefs about all the things she didn't know and couldn't do, and simply commit to dive in and figure it out. In every case, Merriken chose growth over ease, and eventually sold her company to General Mills for over $55M. Today millions of Lärabars are sold around the country every year.

The jump to the next level—whatever that is for you personally—will test your resolve and give you the opportunity to ask again and again, "How bad do I want to grow?" I hope your answer is always, "Bad enough."

EXERCISES FOR GROWTH

1. Where are you hungry for growth? What do you want to accomplish?

2. What beliefs about yourself will you have to give up in order to grow in this way?

3. Create a plan for the passive and massive action you will need to take in order to grow and accomplish what you want.

    a. What is the passive action (information) you need to take in order to reach your goal? Make a list and then schedule each item on your calendar. For example, if you need to learn how to publish a podcast, set specific and limited time aside to learn how to do this, say Friday from 3:00-5:00. Make sure to limit your time. Your brain will want to spend all kinds of days and weeks in passive action.

    b. What are the obstacles your brain is offering to reaching this goal? Make a list of all the excuses your brain is coming up with.

    c. Now create a strategy for overcoming each obstacle.

For example, if you want to create a podcast, but your brain is telling you, you don't know how, your strategy is some passive action. Then your brain offers that you don't have time, or you don't have the right equipment, or it's too hard to get approved by iTunes, or your kids might interrupt, or you don't really know what to say to fill a whole podcast episode.

Do you see how your brain can just go on and on making excuses rather than getting down to massive action? Instead of giving in to its resistance, simply list the obstacle on one side of the paper and list your strategy on the other. When the obstacle arises, simply follow the strategy. (Amazingly, the obstacles rarely actually arise...our brain just likes to pretend things are impossible.)

OBSTACLE	STRATEGY

d. Commit to massive action. This means commit to act until the goal is achieved. Schedule time on your calendar to write and record the podcast. Schedule time to edit. Commit to it as if it has already happened. What can you do today? What can you do to get you closer to your goal? Nothing happens without this important component of MASSIVE ACTION.

There were plenty of moments in Magno's journey when he thought he couldn't keep going, but he always found a way.

Back before he started nursing school, Magno was frustrated with his work at Costco. He felt like his work was meaningless. He said when his father was alive, he would point out the people on the street in Sao Paolo who gathered cardboard for recycling to make a living. His father would point to those collecting the cardboard and tell Magno that if he didn't study or go to school, he would end up picking up cardboard the rest of his life.

"Working at Costco I was moving cardboard and cutting cardboard and putting cardboard on flatbeds and taking cardboard to the bailer. Whenever the bailer would get clogged, they'd call me to push the cardboard through. It was the worst job that nobody wanted to do. I was doing exactly what my father had warned me about—I was picking up cardboard.

"So as hard as it was to keep going, that job motivated me to persist. I didn't want to get stuck there. I wanted to get out so I refused to quit in the middle."

Magno said that even though getting his nursing degree wasn't easy, the process was simple and straightforward. "They give you a list of requirements, it could be 20 classes, maybe more, but at the end of it, you have your degree. There is a path. You just have to stay on it. It's only a matter of sticking with it."

Year after year, Magno persisted. One class at a time he improved his knowledge and his skills. One job at a time he increased his earning capacity and his ability to help others. He didn't give up because the process was long. When he realized his daughter was going to be in first grade by the time he graduated with his nursing degree, he also realized that she would be in first grade at that day in the future, regardless of whether or not he had his degree. The time was going to pass.

Magno used the same strategy as he now worked to earn his master's degree so that he could become a nurse practitioner. All told, it would take Magno 15 years to become a nurse practitioner. The road from unqualified snow shoveler to nurse practitioner was admittedly long. But it didn't matter. Magno decided that he could persist as long as it took to reach his goal.

CHAPTER 10

PERSISTENCE

"A river cuts through rock, not because of its power, but because of its persistence."

-Jim Watkins

I recently bought a gift for my five-year-old son. It was a rock tumbler made by National Geographic. The other day we went out rock hunting together. We hiked out into the desert. The weather was beautiful, the winter sun warming our backs as we picked our way through the prickly foliage and cactus, searching for the perfect rocks to take home to polish. My son filled his hands and his pockets with his stony treasures, delighting over each one, imagining what they would look like when they were smooth and gleaming.

When we got home, I did what I should have done when I bought the tumbler and read the instructions. It turns out that rock polishing is not a quick hobby. When you put the rocks in the tumbler you add coarse grit. As the little machine tumbles and spins, the course grit polishes the rocks. But it takes time.

You start with the coarsest grit and turn on the tumbler for six days or so. Then you add a slightly less course grit and run it for another week. Then another drop in grit, with more days in the rock tumbler. Finally, the finest level of grit is added and you run the tumbler for another eight or nine days. The whole time, meanwhile, the tumbler is going day and night, spinning the grit and the rocks and polishing the stones. All told, it takes about a month of constant tumbling to polish your rocks. (Maybe not the best gift for a five-year-old.)

A RIVER RUNS THROUGH IT

The last time we were at the Grand Canyon, I noticed a display in one of the Visitor Centers. Above a beautiful painting of the Canyon at dusk, was printed a quote by Enos Mills: "Given enough time, nothing is more changeable than rock."

That thought stopped me in my tracks at the time and stuck with me. Because to my five-year-old son, watching the rock tumbler work its magic slowly, invisibly, relentlessly, it seems that rock will never change. And even to me, who has experience with granite buildings and marble floors and diamond rings, it seems like rock is reliably unchanging.

But I know better. After all, I've seen the Grand Canyon firsthand. But even though I understand at least on an academic level the power of persistent effort over time, I've stood above the winding Colorado River, nothing more than a tiny silver thread far below me, in awestruck amazement at what can happen when you just don't stop. Ever.

Put simply, persistence is the quality of not stopping. Now if only not stopping was as easy as it sounds.

Have you heard of those people who win cars by holding their hand on a vehicle longer than anyone else? Stacey Rainey won a Ford Explorer exactly this way, by keeping his hand on the car for over 60 hours. When he recounted the experience he said, "In the beginning, I thought that standing there with my hand on a car would be easy. Turns out, it was one of the hardest mental games that I have ever endured."

And that's the problem. For the mighty Colorado and the National Geographic rock tumbler, there isn't any internal resistance or exhaustion or fear to contend with. They just keep going. For the rest of us, we have several mental and physical challenges to overcome in order to exercise the persistence we need to get the results we want in any area of our lives.

COGNITIVE DISSONANCE

Just like it was for Stacey Rainey, one of the hardest parts about persistence is almost always mental. The difficulty arises because there is a gap between the who you are now and the who you want to become. This is known as cognitive dissonance. The mind does not like to hold two contradictory ideas at the same time and it causes enormous mental discomfort.

For example, if you are doing $50,000 worth of sales, but you want to be a person who does $150,000, your mind does not like simultaneously entertaining these two versions of yourself. It can't reconcile the reality of today with the goals of the future, and so it resists the new version you are offering. Your own brain will try to talk you into giving up the new thoughts and come back to homeostasis. It wants you to just keep believing the old thoughts that produce $50,000 worth of sales and be comfortable.

Part of the reason for this cognitive discomfort is because the brain likes to be right. It has a belief system that says you are a person who does $50,000 in sales. When you offer it a new idea— "I'm actually person that makes $150,000 in sales"—that new thought is confrontational and dangerous to the old belief system. It says that we are wrong and have been wrong for some time, and our brains resists this vigorously.

At this point in our progress, the brain will do everything it can to get you to stop, to quit, and give up. It will produce evidence (and lots of it) about why the new thought is wrong. It will tell you that you don't know how, that you've never done it before, that you might fail and be disappointed. It will tell you that it's too hard, that you're not strong enough or smart enough, that you're fine exactly as you are. It is at this point where persistence is most important.

Persistence towards a goal requires that you stay in this place of mental discomfort as you work your way toward your goal without stopping. The key is to remember that the appearance of cognitive dissonance does not mean something has gone wrong. In fact, every time you've grown and changed and evolved and given up a limiting belief system about yourself, you've had to be in this uncomfortable mental space for a significant period of time. You can simply accept it as part of the process—a necessary ingredient in the persistence pursuit of a goal—and continue on regardless of the mental pain and anxiety it causes.

I recently heard an interview with a famous athletic trainer, Jordan Syatt, who was asked about the biggest mistakes people make with their health and fitness. The trainer didn't hesitate. He said the biggest error we make is jumping from program to program, changing our fitness protocols before they've had a chance to work. In other words, we're not persistent.

He pointed out that everybody just wants instantaneous, immediate results and instead of giving our brains and our bodies time to adjust and respond, we give up. We just decide it's not working and move on to something else.

Again, when our minds are confronted with our current fitness level and we simultaneously have a new fitness goal in mind, the cognitive dissonance between the two versions of ourselves makes us uncomfortable. Our brains resist the new version and start to find lots of evidence for why it's not working, why it's never worked for us, why it shouldn't take this long, why we should just throw in the towel. We start to panic: *Maybe it's the program, or maybe if I tried a different diet or did what so-and-so did, or maybe added more cardio, or maybe ad infinitum.* And we jump from program to program, trying to remove the uncomfortable distance between reality and our goal, when all we really need is to sit with the discomfort and persist.

I remember a few years ago when I started a weight-lifting program, I was shocked that even after six months, you could only tell I had been doing anything different if I was flexing and actually holding a weight in my hands. It was even harder for those around me to tell the progress I was making. I remember sending progress photos to my trainer. I was slowly starting to see progress and was kind of proud of the changes that were happening. Her response to me was, "Well, slow progress is better than no progress." Ouch.

The truth is that whatever kind of goal we are working towards, it takes much longer to see the results than we originally anticipate. As we look around us, perhaps our effort does not seem to equate with our results and too many of us are ready to throw in the towel way too early. But over time as you persist, you can look back and see the massive changes that have taken place.

CLEARLY PERSISTENT

I recently started reading a book called *Atomic Habits* by James Clear. In the book, Clear points out that the progress or the results we are seeing towards our goals are much less important than the direction we are headed. Real progress is not generally the result of huge, immediate changes, but rather the accumulation and the culmination of many, many small things that we do consistently over time. Another author, Darren Hardy, calls this "the compound effect." The little things you do every day, are what add up to the results in your life.

While we often want to refer to people as "an overnight success" this is rarely the case. There is a tipping point for success, a point at which all the things we've been doing pay off and we finally see the effect of all of it.

Clear uses an analogy in the book that I think offers a good mental picture for this phenomenon and may help you stick to your goals. He compares our progress towards our goals to an ice cube that is sitting on a table in a room that is 25° Fahrenheit. If our goal is to melt the ice cube and we slowly heat the room up by one degree to 26°, the ice cube will show no visible change though we have put in serious effort towards melting it.

As we continue to heat the room, one degree at a time—27°, 28°, 29°, 30°—there will still be no visible change for our efforts. Finally, when we reach 32°, we will finally see some progress. We have hit the tipping point and the ice begins to melt. While each degree change along the way did not give us the visible result we were seeking, they were all necessary steps along the way.

Imagine if we had given up around 29°, for example, assuming that "it's not working" or "perhaps we're doing it wrong." Our goal would appear impossible and unattainable, when in reality, we only need to give it more time, persist in our efforts, and wait for the tipping point.

PRACTICE MAKES PERFECT

Once you've come to peace about the mental challenges that persistence requires, you will be better prepared to handle the physical ones. By this I mean, the physical, active work and daily production required to reach your goals.

The first thing to understand is that whatever capacity, skills, or mastery your goals require, acquiring them is more about consistent practice than it is about in-born talent or natural gifts. All skills—whether they are hard skills, like dribbling a basketball or playing the right notes on a violin, or soft skills like reading and responding to a room during a presentation or solving a customer service issue—are a matter of developing the right neuropathways and they can all be developed over time through persistent practice.

As Dan Coyle wrote, "Whatever talent you set out to build, from golfing to learning a new language to playing the guitar to managing a startup, be assured of one thing: You are born with the machinery to transform beginners' clumsiness into fast, fluent action. That machinery is not controlled by genes, it is controlled by you. Each day, each practice session, is a step toward a different future. This is a hopeful idea, and the most hopeful thing about it is that it is a fact."[16]

In order to create these new neural pathways and use the machinery you were born with to create the life you want, there has to be action on your part. Consistent, persistent, unstopping action. Think about those changing rocks again. Both the river and the grit have to keep moving to create the change. Over time, it is *movement* that allows for transformation of the rock.

This means that the kind of action and practice that changes your neurology and eventually your skill set is not just thinking about a goal or reading about a goal or planning to act someday on your goal, but taking genuine, *measurable* action every day— in other words, *practicing* your craft, whatever that is.

For example, if you are working on a hard skill like mastering a cello concerto, this will require repeatable, precise practice that hard wires the brain and makes quick superhighway connections between neurons. It will require deep enough practice to create automatic responses from your fingers and vast amounts of muscle memory that has been laid down note by note over time. Neurologists have determined that creating

---

[16] Coyle, Daniel. *The Little Book of Talent*. N.p.: Bantam, 2012.

efficient neuropathways through accurate practice allows the speed of the connections between neurons to increase from 2 mph to 200 mph!

On the other hand, if you are working on soft skills like improving your sales abilities, action will require you to put yourself in situations where you have opportunities to read, respond and react, not in automatic ways, but in intuitive, creative ways. You will need to practice a pitch, yes, but more importantly you will need to practice what comes after, with all the variables you can't control. As you do it over and over again, improvising and reacting, your brain will develop faster and faster responses.

The more you can put yourself in situations where you can practice this kind of interaction and then get feedback about your performance, the better you will become at any skill. Yes, it will look clumsy and inexpert at first. That's the way it should be. Just be willing to be lousy at it. Then explore with curiosity what works and what doesn't. After each attempt you can think about what you want to repeat and hardwire and what you don't and why. With persistence you will change over time. 100% guaranteed.

In both cases, with hard and soft skill practice, you must allow for error.

Wayne Gretzky's teammates would sometimes see him fall on the ice when doing solitary drills after team practice sessions. While it may seem incongruous for such an expert hockey player to fall like a beginner on new skates, Gretzky was always focused on continuous improvement and pushing the boundaries of his own talent and skills. The only way to build the new neural pathways that would increase his ability was to try new things— to reach and fail until the connections were effectively wired.

You must welcome error as a way to create the brain connections you need to get better at any talent you want to acquire. You have to put yourself out there. There isn't a shortcut that circumvents looking stupid or making mistakes. Again, your brain will wonder why you're doing all this—experiencing so much discomfort, so much humiliation. There's got to be an easier way.

Here's the thing: there's not. The people who achieve what they want, practice until their brains learn the skills required. You want it? You just keep at it. Every practice solidifies another neural connection. Every rep gets you closer to mastery. Persistence is the key to all of it.

A (CHICKEN) WING AND A PRAYER

In 2007 Stacy Brown found herself newly divorced and desperately needing a way to provide for her three small children. When she was a young girl, her father used to ask her what problems she had seen that day and then have her come up with a way to solve them. At this moment in Stacy's life, she had a problem and she needed to solve it...and fast.

She thought about her skills, about what she had to offer the world. Stacy was a pretty good cook and she had a self-proclaimed "passion" for chicken salad. She had a favorite spot to get it in every town she had lived or visited. She considered herself an expert at *eating* chicken salad. She wondered if she could develop the skills to make chicken salad and then sell it in her neighborhood and town.

She decided to try. Thinking about the unique characteristics of each of her favorite chicken salads—the moisture content of one, the texture of another, the flavor of another—she thought she could come up with the perfect chicken salad recipe and sell it to friends and neighbors as a way to make ends meet.

Stacy's goal was to earn $500 a month to be able to provide for her family.

She began by practicing her skills and experimenting with recipes. She started with the chicken. At first, she had no idea what kind of chicken would work best. She said, "It was just like a science experiment. I went through cooking whole chickens on the bone, I cooked chicken breasts on the bone, I cooked boneless breasts, I cooked tenderloins." Everything yielded different amounts and affected the taste of the recipe as well as her food costs. Eventually she developed a method that worked best. She had one hard skill down.

After she found a recipe she liked, she started taking Tupperwares full of chicken salad around town and asking people to try it. She got lots of feedback: Too dry. Too soupy. Too salty. A little bland. Every time she got some feedback, she'd go back to the kitchen and keep tweaking her recipe. She was curious and adaptable.

Finally, one day she said someone took a bite from the Tupperware bowl and they closed their eyes, their head went back, and they made a strange little moan. Bingo. She had her recipe. Another small step towards her goal.

Then she started selling the well-researched, popular chicken salad recipe door-to-door. She put a sticker on her car that said, "Chicken Salad Chick" as advertising and dropped a bowl off at the teacher's lounge at the elementary school along with some business cards. The orders started rolling in. She was getting lots of practice on her chicken salad skills. Maybe a little too much, she admits as she remembers some very late nights crying over bowls and bowls of chicken salad. Stacy Brown was taking massive action towards her goals, and she kept at it.

Just as she was getting overwhelmed by the work, she got a call from Stan at the Lee County Health Department, who told her that what she was doing was illegal. As quick as it had started, it seemed her chicken salad dream was over.

But Stacy persisted.

She and her business partner, Kevin Brown, decided to open a little 800 sq. ft take-out restaurant. They didn't have any money to hire the work on the building, so they took lots of trips to Home Depot and figured out how to build it themselves.

The first day, they sold 40 pounds of chicken salad in two hours, so the next day they decided to double it. They sold all 80 pounds, again in about two hours. For months and months, they continued like this, selling hundreds of pounds of chicken salad every day. The problem was, they weren't making any money.

They needed some different skills and so they started working on those. They just kept moving forward and figuring it out as they went. They streamlined processes and figured out food costs and inventory and how to turn a profit.

Eventually they made enough money to open two other Chicken Salad Chick restaurants. They had to come up with their own funding because no bank would lend to them given their unproven business plan, but they persisted. No matter the challenge, no matter the obstacle, they kept working and their little business kept growing.

A FOX IN THE HEN HOUSE

One of the Chicken Salad Chick restaurants was in Auburn, Alabama, a college town. Whenever visitors came to see their kids or watch a football game, they'd come to Chicken Salad Chick. They started to get lots of franchise requests from people who wanted to take the restaurant to other parts of the South.

But the Browns, who had married by now, didn't know how to set up a company that could support the franchises. Here again, they come up against a skill they didn't have. They decided to partner with another couple that had some franchise experience.

They made some mistakes in setting up the deal. Remember that errors are part of acquiring the skills we need to grow. It was no different for Stacy and Kevin Brown. As is often the case, the learning process proved to be extremely painful.

The most critical error for the Browns was giving this other couple the majority share in their business. Someone else now owned 51 percent of Chicken Salad Chick. When this couple started making decisions and changes that the Browns didn't agree with, the Browns tried to dissolve the partnership. However, the couple pointed out that it wasn't really a partnership. Because they owned 51 percent of the business, they could simply fire the Browns and do whatever they wanted with Chicken Salad Chick. The Browns were devastated.

Luckily, the company had a board of directors. The board determined that because the Browns had started the company, they should be given the option to buy the other couple out and regain full ownership of the company. The other couple agreed— the Browns could buy back their share at three times the price they had sold it for only four months earlier ($1.2M) and it had to be done in 30 days.

THE CHICKENS COME HOME TO ROOST

The Browns spent the next 28 days, persistently and doggedly trying to raise the capital and find investors that would allow them to buy their business back. They called it their Southeastern Fundraising Tour. Again, a whole new set of skills was required. And this time, they were up against the clock.

Stacy says, "We packed up coolers full of chicken salad to hand out to possible investors, and we pitched to anyone that would listen. And at every single meeting we heard, 'You want us to invest this much money for a minority share of a business that does not have a single franchise open. Thanks, but no thanks.' We were laughed out the room."[17]

With only two days left, Stacy remembers sitting on the back porch with her husband when he told her that she was going to have to come to grips with reality. They were going to lose their business. This was the end. And they'd just have to figure out something else.

But Stacy's persistence would not let her give up.

The next day at work, her secretary handed her a slip of paper with five names on it. She told her, "Call these people. It's all I've got. But give them a try."

Stacy called all five of the men and begged them to come listen to one last pitch. The Browns delivered their best pitch, took them to lunch at Chicken Salad Chick, and then as Stacy tells it, "I packed them up, full of coolers of chicken salad, we put them in their cars and we said goodbye to our last chance." They knew it was the end.

But on the way home, they got a call from one of the gentlemen in the meeting, Earlon McWhorter, who asked to meet them back at the restaurant. He said was willing to invest in the Browns and their chicken salad dreams.

With the investment of capital from McWhorter, the Browns bought their business back and began franchising the business. Soon there were restaurants all over the south. By the end of 2018, there were over 100 Chicken Salad Chick restaurants in operation. The little home business that needed to make $500 a month, now makes over $75M dollars in revenue every year.

---

[17] Raz, Guy. "Chicken Salad Chick: Stacy Brown." *How I Built This*. Podcast audio. July 2, 2018. Accessed January 4, 2019. https://www.npr.org/2018/06/29/624713103/chicken-salad-chick-stacy-brown.

CAN'T STOP, WON'T STOP

Over and over again, Stacy Brown had to act. She had to practice skills she didn't have. She had to ignore the cognitive dissonance between where she was and where she wanted to be. She had to persist when giving up and getting a simple 9-to-5 job would have been easier.

Whenever we have the urge or the impulse to quit, it is only because we want out of the feeling we are currently experiencing. Whether that feeling is shame or fear or overwhelm or anger or frustration, persisting means that we are going to have to keep feeling all of it. This is the fundamental difference between people who accomplish their goals and those who don't. Stacy Brown was willing to feel scared and lost and out of her depth over and over again to make her dreams a reality.

The Brown's story of persistence doesn't end there. In 2015, Kevin was diagnosed with Stage 4 colon cancer that had already metastasized to his lungs. With the same persistence and determination with which they had grown their business, the Browns worked to start a charitable foundation with the primary goal of funding research. They organized a benefit concert and filled Jordan-Hare Stadium in Auburn, headlining Kenny Chesney to perform for 50,000 fans as a way to raise funds for the cause.

At this point, they knew they could do anything they decided to do. After all, they had been practicing for years.

Tragically, Kevin Brown lost his battle with colon cancer before the concert took place, but today Stacy Brown fights on for both of them. Her story is one of absolute persistence. She just never stopped. And just like a rock, given enough time and enough action, she changed her life. In her own words, "And when life knocks you down, you just keep getting up." Over and over again.

It's not flashy and it's not magic. It's just work done persistently over time that creates real change for each of us. Remember that for rocks and for people, change is so imperceptibly slow and small it's hard to see up close, but the cumulative effect is truly awe inspiring.

EXERCISES IN PERSISTENCE

Persistence creates changes over time. Given enough time, what could you change or accomplish in your life?

1. Record one goal that keeps tapping at you.

2. What are the feelings that come up when you think about trying to accomplish your goal? Is it fear? Is it shame? Identify the primary emotion that surfaces around this goal.

3. Ask yourself, "Am I willing to feel _____, in order to achieve my goal?"

4. What hard skills do you need to practice to reach your goal? Make a list.

5. What soft skills do you need to practice to reach your goal? Make a list.

6. Ask yourself, "Am I willing to feel _____(#2)_____ for 3 months or 6 months or a year in order to reach my goal?" Really think about the trade-off. Would it be worth it to you? Record why or why not.

7. Finally, choose one skill (from #4 or #5) you are going to practice consistently for 30 days in order to reach your goal. Commit to practicing every day. Log onto the Unqualified Success website and record your commitment. We want to know what you're working on!

8. For 30 days, practice your specific skill. If you miss a day, curiously explore why you missed practice. How can you avoid that obstacle next time?

9. Start again immediately, without shame or blame or regret. Start again and persist. Give it 30 days. See what you can accomplish, given enough time to do it.

After Magno finished all his coursework for his master's degree at Grand Canyon University he still had to write a dissertation in order to earn his nurse practitioner's license.

He had a good friend that was a nurse back in St. Mark's Hospital in Utah, who was working towards the same degree. When this friend went to submit his dissertation, it was not accepted and he never got to graduate or receive his degree to practice as a nurse practitioner. To Magno it seemed like his friend had done a lot of work for nothing. This was a man that Magno looked up to. He admired his skills as a nurse. To know that his friend had not received his degree because his dissertation wasn't approved was very nerve-wracking.

Magno said, "The most intimidating part for me in all my education was my final dissertation—would I be able to accomplish that and finish? I knew I could pass the classes. But the scariest thing for me was doing the final project to write my dissertation."

As well as Magno knew English at this point, he still found writing in English very challenging. It was harder to convey his thoughts through the written word than it was to speak and converse.

Magno became a humble learner as he wrote his final project. He tried to do everything his instructors said. "My goal in life was to please the instructors, to receive approval from my teachers, and do what they wanted me to do because they had the power to pass me or fail me."

Magno followed their guidelines and suggestions as closely as he could. "I never thought I was right or that I was more knowledgeable. It didn't matter if I had spent x number of hours on this dissertation; if a teacher told me to do it again, I would do it again. I did it over and over again. I swallowed my pride and finished my paper."

Throughout his whole life, Magno's willingness to be humble and teachable made a huge difference in his outcome. He was always confident (If you can do it, I can do it), but never prideful. Immediately after thinking, "If you can do it, I can do it," he would ask, "How did you do it?" He never let his pride keep him from asking questions to learn what he needed to know. Magno's vulnerability made him powerful.

CHAPTER 11

VULNERABILITY

"We are at our most powerful the moment we no longer need to be powerful."

— Eric Michael Leventhal

I once heard Oprah Winfrey being interviewed about her career as a talk-show host. She spoke about what she had learned and the powerful lessons she had received by talking to her guests. In the interview, she shared something that I have never forgotten.

She explained how over the years, she had interviewed guests from every walk of life. During her career, she has talked with the most successful people in the world, the most talented and accomplished: titans in every industry, thought leaders, politicians, musicians, athletes. She also interviewed those who have suffered and caused great suffering: cult leaders, criminals, racists, and everything in between. The ordinary as well as the powerful. The poor as well as the wealthy. The seemingly well-adjusted and the apparent messes.

She said the one thing they all had in common is that at the end of the show they all wanted to know the same thing, "Did I do okay?"

Did I do okay? Behind that question sits the subtext: Am I okay? Am I enough? If you approve of me, then I must be okay.

Every human being, no matter what they have accomplished or what their title is or what their goals are, carries a fundamental insecurity within in them that they don't measure up, that their value or worth is always being weighed. The desire to feel okay about who we are and what we do and how other people perceive us is universal, innate, and begins early in life.

Though this built-in vulnerability exists in everyone, we tend to panic when we find it in ourselves. There is an expectation that at some point we will reach a skill mastery, or a job level, or a knowledge threshold, or a confidence ceiling, where we are no longer dogged by self-doubt or insecurity.

First, it's good to know that this is not the case. Self-doubt is part of the human condition. As Catherine Thomas said, "Somewhat as aliens in a world that is inimical to our spiritual natures—we may carry an insecurity, a self-pain that pervades much of our emotional life."

Spending our time thinking we should not feel this way, or that we need to take certain action so that we will never feel this way again, creates a lot of resistance in our lives and we end up wasting a lot of time hiding our vulnerabilities from others. None of this is a good use of our time or energy.

I want to suggest instead, that embracing our vulnerability, rather than avoiding it, is a key element of achieving the success we want.

SECURE IN THE KNOWLEDGE

When we stop trying to prove that we are enough, we open up enough space to learn something new.

I have been snow skiing since I was a child. Every Christmas, my family would head to the slopes and spend a week together riding the lifts and gliding our way down through the powder. The tradition has continued as my brothers and sisters and I have grown up and now we all bring our kids and enjoy the gorgeous, snow-covered slopes for a few days every year.

A few years ago, a few of my nieces and nephews wanted to try snowboarding instead. I decided to join them, excited about the challenge and a new way to get down the mountain. We signed up for lessons and rented our boards.

And then I spent the morning on my butt in the snow. Up and down. Up and down. Up and down, but mostly down. I just couldn't figure out how to shift my body weight and balance on the board. I was baffled and embarrassed.

I kept telling my 20-year-old snowboard instructor, "I'm really good at skiing. I'm not sure what's happening here. I'm really good at skiing." All morning long, I assured him that I was no beginner and, in fact, I am really good at skiing.

Just before lunch, I found myself on my butt yet again. My instructor boarded next to me and said, "I know, I know. You're really good at skiing. But lady, this isn't skiing."

I had been so concerned about not looking like a beginner that I had failed to put my energy toward learning. Ironically, in an effort to avoid looking foolish, I had foolishly wasted an opportunity to gain new skills and learn from someone who knew more than me.

None of us are experts in everything. We all have strengths. We all have strong suits. But if we want to expand our abilities and capacities, we must also accept that we have lots of things left to learn.

Satya Nadella became the Chief Executive Officer at Microsoft in 2014. When he arrived, his first order of business was defusing and changing the competitive, silo-oriented culture that was prevalent in the company. His vision was to create an environment that promoted learning and sharing viewpoints. In an early email he wrote, "I fundamentally believe that if you are not learning new things, you stop doing great and useful things."

Nadella was highly influenced by Carol Dweck's book, *Mindset*, which he had read a few years before becoming the CEO in an effort to address the way his kids were being educated. In the book she talks about how kids at school are either "know-it-alls" and or "learn-it-alls." Ultimately the learn-it-all will be more successful even if the know-it-all starts out with a higher capacity in the beginning. This became the basis of Nadella's personal mantra: learn it all, don't know it all.

What could you learn if you didn't already know it all or have to pretend that you know it all?

Shunryu Suzuki encouraged a philosophy that he called "The Beginner's Mind." Now, none of us want to be a beginner (even when we're snowboarding), but looking at a problem with a beginner's mind allows you to learn new things. In an effort to be efficient, our brain filters "relevant" information from the "irrelevant." When things are familiar, it's easy to stop seeing everything available to us.

But when we use a beginner's mind, the brain now has to take everything in again "for the first time" which enables you to see things that your experienced mind has possibly ignored or discounted. Suzuki said, "In the beginner's mind there are many possibilities, in the expert's mind there are few."

As we let go of our preconceived expectations, and observe with a beginner's mind, new ways of thinking and doing open up. If you experience your life holding the assumption that you already know how it should be done, you won't see what's available to learn. However, if you can look with beginner's eyes, fresh and curious, then the revelations can begin.

WILLING TO SUCK AT IT

Whenever we start something new, set a goal, decide to improve at something, or reach for a dream, self-doubt magically appears. Most of us are surprised. *You're still here? Oh, yes.*

Anytime we decide to move outside our comfort zone, we can confidently expect a visit from our entourage of self-doubt. Doubt moves in packs, you know. They're too scared to go around on their own, so they show up as troupe of "toos": too dumb, too young, too old, too uneducated, too inexperienced, too naïve, too black, too white, too female, too male, too quiet, too loud, too insecure.

What I like to say to my toos is "Too bad. I'm doing it anyway."

Recently I have had the chance to say this a lot. Last year I started a technology company to provide software for restoration companies. Being the CEO of a restoration company is very different than being the CEO of a startup technology company. Everybody that heard I was transitioning into technology gave me advice. They said that I should plan on everything being late, past deadline, never on schedule, and never in budget. I thought maybe that was true for everybody else, but not me.

I soon learned that the communication cycle for the tech development process is very challenging. There's what you have in your head, and it has to go through a business analyst. The business analyst has to give it to the developer and then they have to produce something and bring it back to you.

It's like a really expensive of game of telephone. You send it out one way and it comes back completely different than what you expected. It was difficult to learn how to effectively communicate and exchange ideas with a developer whose mind works completely different than yours as a contractor with experience in the field.

Throughout this process, as I have tried and failed, and tried and failed, instead of just giving up, I have returned again and again to the thought, "What if I was just willing to suck at it?"

At the beginning, I wasn't good at it and I'm still learning, so there are days when I'm probably still pretty bad at it, but I'm willing to do exactly that in order to reach my goals. In the end, we will have a really superior product; but going through the process and learning *while being willing to suck at it for a while* is what is going to create it.

There have been a lot of days and nights where my self-doubt showed up and said, "You know, I don't think I'm cut out to be the CEO of a technology company. I don't have enough knowledge, I don't have enough experience, and half the time I don't know what they're talking about."

But then I remember that I do know restoration really well. I know the customer really well. And I know the end user, all those contractors out there, really well. So if I can be willing to be bad long enough to get better, then I can bridge the gap and create something amazing.

Being willing to suck takes humility and vulnerability and is all the start of any new endeavor requires. That is the only qualification to get better: being willing to suck when you start.

Anne Lamott wrote a brilliant little book on writing called, *Bird by Bird*, that I've read several times. One of my favorite chapters is entitled "Shitty First Drafts." In it, she describes the idea that you have to start somewhere. The only way to get to good is to begin at bad. When you give yourself permission to write a crappy first draft, then the white, blank page isn't so intimidating.

It doesn't matter how bad that first draft stinks, because it's just the starting point. This philosophy—that you don't have to be perfect or even good when you begin—takes all the pressure off. Without this permission, when we start with that empty page and the expectant cursor, we are frozen by self-doubt, wanting it to be perfect (or at least really, really good) and yet we don't know how to do that yet.

The how is the crappy first draft. And I'm here to tell you that the crappy first draft philosophy works in any area of your life.

Do you want to build your business? Allow yourself to try some things that might look like the equivalent of a terrible first draft. Do you want to become a really good cook, or learn Mandarin, or become a foster parent, or invest your money? Give yourself permission to do it badly at first. Do you want to have a better marriage, or uplevel your listening skills, or learn to how to create Facebook ads that convert? Be willing to suck at it. You can do anything if you're willing to be bad at it when you start.

LEARN, UNLEARN, AND RELEARN

When our brain first learns something, it has to create a new neuropathway in order to be able to access the new information. This takes time and work. The more the brain uses the neuropathway, the faster the connection fires and the more automatic the response becomes.

Maybe you have had the experience of moving or changing jobs within your same town. A few years ago my parents moved out of my childhood home. I would find myself automatically driving to their old neighborhood, only to have to turn around and go to the new house. I had to concentrate deliberately for a week or two about which turns to make to arrive at the new house. Eventually the new neuropathway to the new home became as automatic as the old one.

So much of what you do every day, is done quickly and automatically because it is deeply programmed into established neuropathways. You don't have to think about every step and every component involved. You don't have to think about how to turn the coffee on or put the toothpaste on the toothbrush or what to put in the lunch sacks. Your brain has it wired.

When we are babies our brains are on overdrive, creating new neuropathways and automating as much as possible to be as efficient as possible. My brother, Christian was born deaf. His brain never received any electrical signals from the stereocilia in his ear and so those neuropathways were never established. He never learned "how to hear" or interpret the sounds around him.

When he was 16, he received a cochlear implant, that effectively took the place of those cilia and started sending electrical impulses to the brain. I remember after his surgery we all gathered around expectantly. The doctor turned on the cochlear implant and we started animatedly talking to him, "Can you hear? Can you hear?" He looked confused and signed, "I don't know. Is this hearing?"

His brain had no neuropathways built for interpreting the electrical signals the implant was now sending to his brain. Those would have to be built by the brain, one-by-one, just as if he was a baby learning to hear.

I remember watching him when he would get home from school. He would sit down on the couch, close his eyes, turn off the implant, and then take a deep sigh. He didn't want to be bothered by anybody. He was exhausted. He had never heard before. The brain didn't know what sounds to ignore and what sounds to pay attention to. It was just a constant stream of signals that didn't make any sense. He had no way to interpret the signals because the pathways weren't established or fast enough yet to be understandable. It was almost excruciating for him to wear the device.

Whenever we decide to learn something new, we all go through this same, somewhat excruciating, process. We have to work much harder than we're used to. We have to concentrate like we are unaccustomed to doing. Brain work is hard work and that is why doing new things and going outside of our comfort zone makes us vulnerable. None of it is automatic and we don't yet have the neuropathways established to allow us to feel natural or confident.

However, over time the brain adjusts. The new neuro-highways get built and the signals move along these new paths just as fast as the old ones. The more the connections are used, the faster they get. Pretty soon, it is automatic.

The challenge for each of us that want to improve and uplevel our lives, is that in the areas where we want to grow, we sometimes already have established ways of doing things that are ingrained in deep neuropathways. We make our sales calls the same way. We give presentations in the same format. We exercise the same muscles every morning. We treat our family members the same way we always have.

Many years ago, I read an article by Marcia Conner in *Fast Company*, and she shared a story that has stuck with me. She said that one summer she was doing door-to-door sales. She had a standard pitch that she would always lead with. Her brain had an established neuropathway that it fired over and over again as she gave her spiel.

She said that one day her boss told her to put a piece of bologna in one of her shoes. Even though this seemed crazy, she did as she was instructed. She wrote, "At the first house we visited, I physically couldn't say my opening the same way. The bologna distracted me enough so that I needed to reflect on e-v-e-r-y word. The next day, without the bologna, my approach was still fresh, engaging, and more successful than it had been two days before. I had unlearned, and I had relearned."[18]

Sometimes, by really examining the results we are getting in our lives, we can see exactly where we can benefit from unlearning a few things and establishing new neuropathways in their place.

OPEN TO CHANGE

Serena Williams was the top-ranked female tennis player in the world at the start of the 2010 tennis season. But during a tournament in Munich she stepped on some broken glass at a restaurant after a match and had to sit out the rest of the season while she healed.

She came back in the middle of 2011, but she didn't participate in a few of the Grand Slam tournaments, lost a few times, and her ranking slipped to 12th. In 2012, her downward trajectory continued when she lost in the French Open. The New York Times wrote about her loss as "an upset that ranked among the most stunning and unexpected in recent history."

Serena was plagued by self-doubt and insecurity. She was training harder than ever, but nothing seemed to be working correctly.

Following the shocking defeat in the French Open, Serena searched for help. She went to Patrick Mouratoglou's academy. After Patrick watched her practice, he gave her his assessment: "Every time you hit, you are off balance, which makes you miss a lot," he told her. "Also, you lose power because [your] body

---

[18] Connor, Marcia. "Learn, Unlearn, and Relearn." *Fast Company*, February 27, 2006. Accessed December 10, 2018. https://www.fastcompany.com/919166/learn-unlearn-and-relearn.

weight doesn't go through [the shots], and you're not moving up, so your game is slow."[19]

Now, Serena knew how to play tennis. She knew how to play tennis at the highest level. She had won the biggest Grand Slams in the world. She could have walked away, discounted Mouratoglou's comments, satisfied that she knew at least as much as he did. But instead, Serena said, "Let's work on it."

That kind of vulnerability and openness, especially at Serena's level of expertise and accomplishment is rare. But it made a world of difference for Serena Williams.

They worked together for a week, speeding up Serena's footwork so that she could set up faster in order to hit the ball faster. Serena set aside her own ideas and former training and fully embraced Mouratoglou's coaching and new techniques. Then Serena went home to the United States to get ready for Wimbledon.

Just before Wimbledon, Williams announced that Mouratoglou would be her new coach. After years of working one way that had been highly successful, she was willing to learn in a new way with a new coach.

After that, Serena won both Wimbledon and the U.S. Open, her next 19 matches, as well as a gold medal at the 2012 Summer Olympics. She was willing to be vulnerable and take a huge risk in order to continue to excel in her tennis game and it paid off big time.

Especially when we have had a measure of success, many of us are reluctant to consider that there might be more to learn, that there might be a way to improve our game, that we still have

---

[19] O'Reilly, Barry. "The Power of Unlearning: Serena Williams' Story." Singularity Hub. Last modified January 18, 2019. Accessed January 29, 2019. https://singularityhub.com/2019/01/18/ the-power-of-unlearning-serena-williams-story/#sm.0011c9cs718ascpyx8z2mcsfda59y.

room to grow and progress. We are often hesitant to take this course of vulnerability because the outcomes and results are unknown and that innate insecurity we carry begs us not to expose ourselves.

When we are willing to trade our need to win or succeed for a need to simply learn and grow instead, we open another world of possibility for achievement. Don't let either your successes or your failures hold you back from the things that are available for you to learn.

RELAXING OUR GRIP

When we feel unqualified or vulnerable in any area of our lives, we tend to tighten up and operate out of fear. We set goals only to make ourselves feel better about ourselves and we improve in an effort to outrun our vulnerability.

In this mindset, we are desperate to achieve our goals if only to feel, for a moment, that we are enough. When we operate like this, we grit our teeth and latch onto our goals with an anxious stranglehold. We need results and we need them fast.

This doesn't leave any room for the magic to happen. We can't be patient with the universe, or God, or ourselves, or anybody on our team. We can't move methodically from rough draft to second draft to final draft, making steady but unremarkable improvement. We can't work systematically on our footwork and then our balance and then our follow-through because we just have to have the win. We also can't access our creativity or find inspiration because we're too afraid of making a mistake on the narrow, treacherous road to our goal.

Steve Jobs was fired from Apple in 1985. Later, he reflected, "I didn't see it then, but it turned out that getting fired from Apple was the best thing that could have ever happened to me. *The heaviness of being successful was replaced by the lightness of being a beginner again*, less sure about everything. It freed me to enter one of the most creative periods of my life."

Being fired made Steve Jobs less sure and vulnerable. It allowed Jobs to relax his grip enough renew his relationship with his creativity. Though being fired may not be on your list of goals, we can all access "the lightness of being a beginner again" that Williams and Jobs were able to experience as a way to learn, expand our creativity, and remove the roadblocks to our goals.

This does not mean that we relax in taking action. We can always be taking massive action toward a goal. What we need to relax is our dependence on a certain result in an attempt to erase our vulnerability or cover an inadequacy. We are always working hard toward our goals—Serena Williams was thinking and training in a new way, but working as hard or harder than ever—but when we embrace our vulnerability, we are open to the learning, the development, and the magic that can happen along the way.

PUT YOUR HANDS UP AND STEP AWAY FROM THE GOAL

It may seem counterintuitive to relax on your way to the goal. Remember, you aren't relaxing *your effort*. You are relaxing *your need for a particular result.*

The prefrontal cortex part of your brain is in charge of problem solving. When you are trying to find a solution, come up with a new idea, or progress towards your goal, your brain is engaged and working hard. But keep in mind that the prefrontal cortex is also in charge of accessing the other existing information and experiences you have stored away in your memory.

When you are focused on a task, trying to solve a problem or work towards a goal, the brain is busy and doesn't have time to make connections with all the information you have stored away. However, when we let up briefly and do an automatic task like take a shower, do the dishes, or take a walk, the brain is then free to go to work, using all your stored memory and information along with the new input to find solutions to your problems.

Marily Oppezzo and Daniel Schwartz, at Stanford, performed a series of four studies where they had students come up with creative solutions to problems either when sitting at a desk or taking a walk. They found creativity increased more than 60 percent when the students were walking rather than sitting.[20]

Oppezzo wrote, "A lot of people think of creativity as a trait, but we found that everyone can improve their creativity with this simple strategy." Allowing your automatic neuropathways to take over for a while gives your brain time to go to work on the problems at hand.

In the final experiment Oppezzo and Schwartz ran, students were asked to generate a creative analogy or metaphor when they were given a statement like "a candle burning low is like_____." Ninety-five percent of those students who walked were able to create at least one, original, high-quality analogy compared to only 50 percent of the students who sat while generating the metaphor—almost twice as much and almost a 100 percent success rate.

IT ALL ADDS UP

Henri Poincaré was a French physicist and mathematician whose work laid the foundation for the theory of relativity as well as four new, modern branches of mathematics. In 1910, he

---

[20] Oppezzo, Marily, and Daniel Schwartz. "Give Your Ideas Some Legs: The Positive Effect of Walking on Creative Thinking." *Journal of Experimental Psychology Learning Memory and Cognition* 40, no. 4 (April 2014).

published an article called *Mathematical Creation*, in which he talked about working as hard as he could on some of the most complex mathematical problems of his day, only to find the solutions when he set them aside for a moment.

He wrote, "For fifteen days I strove to prove that there could not be any Fuchsian functions. Every day I seated myself at my work table, stayed an hour or two, tried a great number of combinations and reached no results. [...] One day, going along the street, the solution of the difficulty which had stopped me suddenly appeared to me. I had all the elements and had only to arrange them and put them together. So I wrote out my final memoir at a single stroke and without difficulty."[21]

Fascinated by this phenomenon which he witnessed over and over again in his work he concluded, "Often when one works at a hard question, nothing good is accomplished at the first attack. Then one takes a rest...and then all of a sudden the decisive idea presents itself to the mind. It might be said that the conscious work has been more fruitful because it has been interrupted and the rest has given back to the mind its force and freshness."

The "freshness" that Poincaré noticed reminds me of the "lightness" that Jobs spoke of a century later. Allowing our minds to rest and undertake some unconscious, automatic activity, frees it up to make the connections we need to have breakthroughs in our careers, in our creative work, and in any of our goal achievement.

All of this is not just magic, of course. Inspiration is always proceeded by real work towards a goal. However, giving our mind time to produce the solutions, allowing space for our brain to figure out "the how," and being vulnerable enough to wait for all of it, is critical to our success.

---

[21] Poincaré, Henri. "Mathematical Creation." *The Monist* 20 (July 1, 1910).

Too many times we let our self-doubt and insecurity convince us that we aren't doing enough, that we're not talented enough, or that we just don't have the ability. None of that is true. Work and wait. Bust your butt and then be vulnerable. Whenever you put in the work and have the courage to wait for the results, it will pay off. I love how Poincaré said it:

> *"...Of a certainty it is only fruitful, if it is on the one hand preceded by a period of conscious work.* These sudden inspirations never happen except after some days of voluntary effort which has appeared absolutely fruitless and whence nothing good seems to have come, *where the way taken seems totally astray.* These efforts then have not been as sterile as one thinks; *they have set agoing the unconscious machine and without them it would not have moved and would have produced nothing."*

Trust yourself enough to approach your life and your goals with vulnerability and a willingness to learn, and then make room for the magic.

EXERCISES IN VULNERABILITY

1. What are some things you find yourself avoiding?

Pick one of the above and answer the following questions about it:

2. Why do you think you avoid this?

3. We only avoid things because we're afraid of how it will make us feel. What is the emotion you are actually trying to avoid?

4. What would change if you believed you could handle feeling that way?

5. Are you willing to be vulnerable enough (feel this feeling) in order to get what you want? Why or why not? Take a curious look at your thinking.

6. List one vulnerable thing you are willing to do this week, regardless of results. Do it(!) and the share your experience on our website.

Magno Santos kept showing up in his life and over time he started to make consistent, steady progress in lots of areas—in his knowledge, in his earning potential, in his ability to contribute in a meaningful way. Everything he did might be considered "small" or unnoteworthy, but it all added up.

Over time, he moved from $1 an hour to $4 an hour to $7 dollars an hour to $11 dollars an hour to $16. He didn't wait around until his wage was "worth his time" or refuse to work until he could be paid "what he deserved." At school, he moved from a general associate's degree to RN to BSN to MSN to FNPC. He just kept continually moving, almost imperceptibly but also inexorably, toward his goals.

After Magno received his second associate's degree from Salt Lake Community College, the first in general studies and the second in nursing, he decided to keep going and earn his bachelor's degree in nursing. But when he went to apply, they said he couldn't get a bachelor's degree because he didn't have a high school diploma.

Despite having two associate's degrees, he couldn't move on to get his nursing bachelor's degree without first going backward to get a high school diploma. So Magno showed up again and went backwards. After looking at his college transcripts, the high school was able to match up all of his general college classes with the requirements for a high school diploma except for one: he still needed geography. Magno took the books home and studied geography and then came back to take yet another test to get his high school diploma. Whatever was required, Magno showed up and did it.

It seemed like whatever Magno wanted to do, there were hoops he had to jump through. Rather than give up or resist, Magno just showed up and jumped through them. One at a time.

When Magno was originally accepted into Grand Canyon University's master's program, he couldn't enroll in classes right away because of his job and his house and everything he had to put in order in Utah. The school told him they would save his spot for 2010. Magno went home and made preparations to come to Arizona.

He sold his house. He quit his job. He moved his family. However, when he finally arrived in Phoenix, the school said that the requirements had changed since he had been admitted and now he would have to go through an interview process. Magno explained that he had already been admitted. But the school insisted that he had to have an interview anyway.

Magno recalled, "I was willing to do the interview, but I was already living here. I moved to Arizona in January 2010, and my interview wasn't until February or March."

Magno didn't want to wait to get started. Instead, he told the professors and doctors at GCU, "Look, I am committed to this. I had my dream job in Utah. In my life, I started as a CNA, became an LPN, then an RN. I became the house supervisor at the hospital and I was in the best position that I could be in, but I wanted to be here, to come to your school.

"I'm already here, I moved here, I left my job to be at your school. And now you tell me, I can't come in unless I pass an interview. I'm here now. You don't get more committed than me."

Essentially, he told the admissions committee: "I show up. I always show up. And I will show up here in this program as well." His pattern of commitment, consistency, and hard work produced results could not be overlooked.

Magno said that after he finished, one of the doctors looked at the others and said, "I think we want him."

We often think only big efforts are worth our time and energy. We concentrate on the big wins and erroneously assume the little stuff isn't that big of a deal. In our impatience to reach our audacious goals, it's easy to overlook and underestimate the power of slow, steady, continuous improvement.

But it turns out that it's only the little stuff that counts after all. The way we do anything is the way we do everything. It's how we show up in our lives every ordinary, average day that makes the difference.

CHAPTER 12

SHOWING UP

"The willingness to show up changes us. It makes us a little braver each time."

— Brené Brown

I think it's fair to say that the marathon is as much a mental race as a physical one. But, the conditions of the 2018 Boston Marathon took that mental game to a whole other level.

With temperatures in the 30s, an icy, pouring rain deluging the course, and headwinds that gusted over 30 mph, racers said there were moments when completely blinded by the rain, it felt like you were just running in place. Hypothermia was a real concern along the entire course.

Desiree Linden won the marathon that day. She was the first American woman to win the Boston marathon since 1985, 33 years earlier. After the race she said, "My hands were freezing, and there were times when you were just stood up by the wind. It was comical how slow you were going, and how far you still had to go."[22] Indeed, the winners for both the men and women posted winning times slower than the course has seen since the 1970s.

---

[22] Butler, Sarah Lorge. "Desiree Linden Wins One for the Pluggers." *Runner's World*, April 16, 2018. Accessed February 25, 2019. https://www.runnersworld.com/news/a19833572/ desiree-linden-wins-one-for-the-pluggers/.

With conditions so miserable, and feeling broken by the weather, Linden said she wanted to drop out after a couple of miles. She argued with herself all through the early miles of the course and tried to justify quitting by thinking "it just wasn't her day." Though tempted to drop out early, her long-practiced work ethic and habit of showing up made her push forward. She thought even if it wasn't her race, maybe she could help one of her fellow Americans. That day Linden ended up assisting two other runners, Shalane Flanagan and Molly Huddle, allowing them to draft and catch up to the pack.

Linden won that day in Boston, but what makes her so special is the way she showed up mile after mile for years and years before that.

GOING ALL IN

Desiree Linden was a pretty fast runner in high school. She won a lot of races, even beating the senior boys on her high school team when she was only a freshman. She won easily at conference meets, but the top spots in the state championships were never hers. She made the top 10, but never ended up in the winner's circle.

It was a similar story for Linden as a runner at Arizona State. She was All-American in both cross-country and track but never came close to winning an NCAA title. Her coach, Walt Drenth told her, "You know, if you take this seriously, you can be pretty good at it." Linden had some talent, but she wasn't really all in.

"I felt like I was pretty good for not being a full-time runner," Linden says. "I could do workouts with Amy [Hastings], with Victoria Jackson, people who were winning national championships. I thought if I committed to it 100 percent, maybe I could be just as good."

For Linden, that decision came after graduation. She had the thought to join the Hansons-Brooks Distance Project, which runs in Rochester Hills, Michigan. Truthfully, she didn't have a lot of options after college. The highest podium she made was a third-place finish in the PAC-10 conference championships running the 5000 meter.

When she tried to contact the Hansons about joining the team, she didn't get a reply. "I knew my credentials weren't incredible," she recalls, "but I was kind of like, 'what's the deal?'" She finally talked to Kevin Hanson, who was noncommittal. He told her if she wanted to come out and visit, she could.

"We negatively recruited her," remembers Keith Hanson. "She's coming out of California and Arizona. She has no idea what the weather's like in Michigan. We don't get snowdrifts like Buffalo—actually the winters are pretty mild here—but it's not the desert Southwest. To have success here, you've got to deal with obstacles. It may take six years of ups and downs, and the people we bring out have to be motivated enough to deal with that."[23]

When Desiree flew to Detroit, the Hanson brothers emphasized the hardships ahead: the winters, the questions from family and friends about the trajectory of her life. "You're going to have a lot of years of putting in mileage that nobody sees," Keith told her. "People won't know your name. It can take five or six years. This is what it is."

Desiree looked right back at him. "I know what it is," she said. "I still want to be a part of it."

"Okay," Kevin told her. "We'll give it a try. We'll see."

---

[23] Barcott, Bruce. "She Can Do It!" Runner's World. Last modified December 28, 2011. Accessed January 25, 2019. https://www.runnersworld.com/races-places/a20805033/desiree-davila-can-do-it/.

It was the first time in her life Desiree Linden put everything into running. "Once...you decide, 'This is what I'm doing,' you invest fully," she says. It was time for Desiree Linden, the runner, to show up.

This was the beginning of Desiree Linden's journey from unspectacular, middle-distance runner to being one of the top marathoners in the world. Six years later, Linden would finish the 2011 Boston Marathon only two seconds behind the winner, an East African runner.

How did she do it? By showing up. By committing and then doing the work that commitment required. As Bruce Barcott wrote, "In six years, [she] went from the third-fastest runner on a PAC-10 team to the third-fastest American female marathoner of all time. That's no miracle. It's a transformation that came about through thousands of mornings and 10,000 miles on a creek-side trail north of Detroit."

As Desiree herself said, "Running is just you, the work you put in, and the clock. You can't cheat yourself. If you don't put in the miles, you can't go to the starting line thinking you're going to pull a miracle out of nowhere. You get out exactly as much as you put in."

And she puts in a lot. At least 90 miles a week for two months before starting her official race buildup, which consists of over 120 miles a week for at least four weeks. If you're keeping track, that's thousands of miles. She doesn't taper much either, knocking her miles down to a mere 90 miles the last 10 days before race day. Day after day, mile after mile, Desiree Linden puts her feet on the pavement and shows up.

BLUE COLLAR RUNNER

When Desiree Linden crossed the finish line in Boston in 2011, just two seconds behind the winner, the commentators were shocked. Who was this and where did she come from? Seven years after that, as she ran the final stretch to the 2018 Boston finish line, Paul Swangard who was commentating the race for NBC Sports labelled her "a blue-collar kind of runner" suggesting to the audience that while not a spectacular runner or an extraordinary talent, Linden was a hard worker who got the job done.

Even after winning that day and finishing nearly four minutes ahead of the next racer, Linden's underestimation continues. As Linden tries to become the first American woman to make three Olympic marathon teams, the skeptics are quick to point out that Linden didn't really win that day in Boston as much as she just survived the weather and there are plenty of writers betting against her Olympic bid for the Tokyo games. Two years out, Robert Johnson recently wrote, "Linden is very consistent and a grinder, but I just don't think her ceiling is as high as the others."

In response to the criticism, Linden shrugs it off. "People say, 'You're a super hard worker' and that's probably better anyways, so I'm fine with it." And as writer Sarah Butler points out, "She's also used to it. She's been hearing that her whole life."[24]

RISE AND GRIND

In Linden's case, her critics are quick to discount the power she produces through her commitment to show up and do the work. It's not flashy. It's not sexy. It's not miraculous. It's just showing up. You will find as you do your own work in the world, that this critique will surface again and again. In a world obsessed with

---

[24] Butler, Sarah Lorge. "Des Linden Won Boston After a Decade of Close Calls—But She's Not Done Yet." *Runner's World*, October 23, 2018. Accessed February 25, 2019. https://www.runnersworld.com/runners-stories/a24066904/des-linden-boston-marathon-winner-training/.

discovering phenomenal talent, there is very little attention paid to the quiet, continuous act of showing up.

Jerry Rice is considered one of the greatest wide receivers to ever play in the NFL. When Bo Eason got traded to the San Francisco 49ers, he played on Jerry's team. Up until that point Bo had a deal with himself that he had made when he was just a boy. He had promised himself that every time he had a practice, he would be the first one on the field and the last one to leave. He said he kept that promise for 20 straight years until he got traded to the 49ers.

On the first day of training camp, Eason arrived early and walked out onto the field expecting to be the first guy out. Eason said, "I'm walking out to the field, I look over and who's out there? Jerry Rice. It doesn't make sense, does it? The greatest football player ever is out there before me? An hour later, everybody else is out there."

Now it's impossible to tell where the line between raw natural talent and hard work begins and ends, but it's possible that Jerry Rice is one of the best to play the game because he's the first to show up and not just because of whatever genetic gifts he received at birth.

The question or all of us is: How committed are you to showing up? How willing are you to show up early, to stay late, to put your feet in the shoes and your shoes on the pavement? What can happen to you over time, just by going all in and showing up?

In 2011, Bruce Barcott of Runner's World wrote, "The Hansons' formula can be boiled down to a sentence: Grind, and live with grinders. It's simple group psychology. 'If you're living with other runners, all devoted to the same thing, then this life you're leading becomes acceptable behavior,' says Kevin Hanson. 'You're not out there all alone, second-guessing all the time you're committing, trying to justify your life choices to others who might not understand.'"

In this little paragraph are some serious nuggets of wisdom for all of us who want to show up more fully and committed in any area of our lives.

First, grind. This is just pure, unadulterated work. You get up, you do your work. Whether or not you feel like it. Whether or not the weather's good. Whether or not you're the best one or the worst one on the team. When we're grinding, nothing else matters but the work itself.

As we've already noted, as humans, we desperately like to believe (no matter what our goal is) that "there has to be an easier way." We are always looking for the easy route to where we are going. This is not because we are inherently lazy, flawed, or defective people. Because our brains are pre-programmed to seek pleasure, avoid pain, and conserve energy, they always like to look for simple, fun, painless ways to accomplish our goals. Unfortunately, these are not the topmost characteristics of any of the worthy goals in our lives.

In order to grind, to show up, to do the work, we are going to have to overcome those natural tendencies for ease and comfort. It's important to be aware that showing up is never what we want to do in the moment. For those of us who want to get to the next level, we just do it anyway. As my dad used to say, "You don't have to want to. You just have to do it."

Be aware that other human beings watching your suffering will try to discourage you, mostly as an act of compassion. They will also insist that there has to be an easier way. They will offer suggestions that maybe "you're trying too hard" or "maybe you should do something that comes more naturally" or even "you're a hard worker, but sometimes that's not enough." Well, I and Desiree Linden are here to tell you that being a hard worker is always enough.

When I was running high school track and cross-country, I earned the same award every year: "Hardest Worker." It was kind of a joke. I was never the fastest or the most naturally gifted. I didn't have the best stride or make it to the podium at the state championships. But I was out there every morning and every night, putting in the miles—my coaches probably thought, "Well, geez, she just keeps showing up. We've got to give her something." And so there it was: "Hardest Worker."

In the end that might be the only award that really counts, because it's the one thing that I can always control. I can't control the markets or the weather or the regulations in my industry, but I can always control how hard I work. I always get to decide if and how I show up. And it's no different for you. It's entirely up to you.

NO WAY AROUND BUT THROUGH

In his world-famous book, *Outliers: The Story of Success*, Malcolm Gladwell builds the premise that there aren't any shortcuts to success. After looking at examples of "the outliers," the people in our societies who have achieved incredible things, he concludes that it was no accident. The people that we look at and hold up as examples of accomplishment and talent have simply put in enormous amounts of work. His theory asserts that anyone who happens to be really good at what they do, didn't just wake up like that. You only see them on game day. You didn't see the 10,000 hours of work and practice that went into the performance.

"There is no way around hard work," Gladwell said in an interview. "There are never any shortcuts, and anyone who tells you there's a shortcut is blowing smoke."[25]

---

[25] Hess, Abigail. "Malcolm Gladwell: There are no shortcuts to success—here's what will up your chances." CNBC Make It. Last modified July 25, 2017. Accessed December 4, 2018.

Gladwell himself was fired from his first writing job because he failed to show up. Quite literally. "I was 20 years old and I couldn't wake up before 11 o'clock in the morning," he admitted. "I have learned many things subsequently, but you know, one of them is the importance of discipline."

Gladwell gives example after example from Bill Gates to the Beatles, from business to the arts and everything in between, that strenuous work is the key to success. It's important to note these achievements from the outside just look like luck. There's enough chance and risk involved that it seems like magic.

Remember that while there is always risk when you put your work into the world that it might not work or it might not be appreciated, showing up is the best way to manage those risks. As Gladwell noted, "Hard work is what makes risk-taking possible. You can't do one without the other. The only way you overcome the obstacles associated with risk-taking is if you put your nose to the grindstone."

GUILT BY ASSOCIATION

The next point in the Hansons' training philosophy Bruce Barcott noted was "live with grinders."

On your way to your goals, you're going to get plenty of feedback, much of it from well-meaning people. They will kindly point out that you are "too focused" or "a little extreme" or maybe "misguided and naïve."

And it's no wonder. Living fully committed does not come naturally, as we've already talked about. Going all in and really showing up does look "extreme" in many cases. It can even

---

https://www.cnbc.com/2017/07/24/heres-what-malcolm-gladwell-learned-after-being-fired-from-his-first-job.html.

appear "unnecessary." Why can't you just be content? You're making the rest of us look bad.

Though not necessary, it can be extremely helpful and bolstering to regularly associate with other people who are also fully committed to showing up in their lives. As Kevin Hanson explained, "You're not out there all alone, second-guessing all the time you're committing, trying to justify your life choices to others who might not understand."

When I went back to work after having my children, I got lots of this kind of "helpful feedback" and judgment, as people wondered why family life "wasn't enough for me." You don't need other people to understand or agree with your goals. Technically, that's your job. When you make a commitment to yourself (and no one else) about the way you will show up in order to achieve your goals, that really is enough to do the work. But it can also be empowering to associate and be a part of a small team of people who have adopted the same modus operandi. You will elevate each other as you show up day after day to do your work in the world.

In my company, we have created a culture that encourages exactly this. We have all set goals that stretch us and require an all-out commitment. When I don't feel like it, I do it anyway, yes. But it's also nice to have a team that reminds me: You've got this. Build a team of like-minded grinders around you and you'll be amazed at what you can simultaneously accomplish.

GRINDING, LITERALLY

Bob Moore got his first job when he was a young teenager. Most of the working-age men were at war and he found himself a department head at age 16. Over his life, he worked for various companies, owned his own gas station, lost everything when he tried to relocate, and then got fascinated by a book about grinding wheat on a stone mill.

The idea of grinding pure grain into flour took hold. Bob Moore thought about the idea constantly. Through a series of events he even acquired three old, 19th-century mill stones from a mill that was being torn down in North Carolina, which he then kept in his garage. Eventually he was able to find a space and start a small mill in Redding, California. All the while, as he opened his mill and a little store front, he worked at Sears to pay the bills.

When Bob was about 50, he decided to enroll in a seminary in Portland to learn how to read the Bible in its original languages. One day as he was out walking with his wife, practicing vocabulary, he saw an old mill with a FOR SALE sign.

Recalling, Bob said, "Basically, I bought the thing and changed my entire life."

In 1978, Bob Moore started his company, Bob's Red Mill and began grinding to build a business out of whole grains. Bob said, "I gave myself three months to the day to get the doors open. And I began a concerted effort to do what I thought I was capable of doing with this building. The building was everything."

Fully committed to his mill and this new way of life, Bob Moore put everything he had into attracting customers. "Every Tuesday the food ads came out in the local paper and I'd put in a two-column article: 'The Mill is Now Running. Come and Enjoy Fresh Stone-Ground Wheat Flour.' I'm a pretty good shouter," he said. "I can yell it out pretty loud and make it work pretty well. Within two weeks of opening the mill I was on the evening news. And then I could fill a parking lot in no time."

Eventually he had local buyers from Fred Meyers, Safeway, and Albertsons, who came to the mill asking to put his products in their stores.

But 10 years after Bob opened the mill, it was destroyed in an arson fire. Only the mill stones were able to be saved. Moore, who was then 60, rebuilt the mill and kept the business open in the meantime by using his warehouse across the street and grinding grain at night in his son's mill in Redding and then driving the flour back to Oregon.

When he was asked what made the difference for him as he built his business, if he was just lucky or if it was something else, he said, "I've always worked hard. I'm crazy. Here I am almost 90, I get up at six every morning. I go down to my own store, my own restaurant, and have cereal. And then, I work until five or six every day. I've always worked hard. So, if working hard is a secret to success, I've done that. I know what it feels like and I probably will never do anything different."[26]

Today Bob's company produces over 400 different products using the same three mill stones from the 1800s and sells them in stores around the world. It employs over 500 people and earns revenues well over $50M annually, none of which Bob Moore ever imagined was even possible.

All because Bob Moore kept grinding. He kept showing up, when his business failed, when he was living with his family in a one room apartment with no shower and no bed, when a fire destroyed his mill, and when buying three old mill stones seemed like the craziest thing in the world to do. It turns out, that contrary to popular opinion, there is no ceiling for those who consistently show up and grind.

---

[26] Raz, Guy. "Bob's Red Mill: Bob Moore." *How I Built This*. Podcast audio. May 21, 2018. Accessed January 10, 2019. https://www.npr.org/2018/05/17/612108005/bobs-red-mill-bob-moore.

RESULTS ORIENTED

The thing that is critical to remember in all of this is that anyone who has put in the work and achieved a measure of success started exactly where you are. We tend to look at "the achievers" and think, "Well, of course they showed up. Look at their life. It's amazing. If I got results like that, I'd show up too."

Understand that when they made their commitment and decided to show up, failure was just as likely as success. They didn't know the result. In many ways, they could not foresee or control the result. They could only control themselves in the present, unglamorous, unnotable moment. And they went to work. Regardless of the outcome. This is the key to showing up. They aren't showing up for the result. They are showing up to show up. When we finally get there, everything changes.

Too many of us have been conditioned to expect a reward for showing up, an immediate result. We start going to the gym, expecting our bodies to change overnight. We take on extra projects at work, in hopes of being noticed or commended. We give everything we have to our children, expecting to be appreciated. We volunteer in our communities, so that we can be admired or respected. When we move our focus from showing up to get whatever we think it will do for us (outside results) to showing up because of what will happen to us in the process (internal results), then real growth, change, and achievement are possible.

MINIMUM BASELINE

The reason this shift is so powerful is because showing up becomes about keeping our commitments to ourselves. Yes, we are showing up in the world, but more importantly we are proving to ourselves that we can be counted on. The more we keep our own word, the more we trust ourselves, the bigger our goals can become.

For many people, as you start to consider the ways you show up in your life, you may find yourself falling short of your own expectations. I want to caution you that your brain will see this as a good time to tell you "who you really are." It will offer that you are just not a morning person, or you are not a go-getter, or you are not competitive, or you are not made like that, or you have never been _____, or you are cautious and conservative, or you are an introvert, or you are a follower and not a leader, ad infinitum. Not only will it have plenty of labels for who you are and who you aren't, it will back up these tidy labels with evidence. File cabinets full.

If there is something in your life that you are not doing that you want to start doing or if there is a place where you are not showing up and doing your work like you want to, the idea of developing "a minimum baseline" can be very useful. It is the beginning step to showing up like you want to—and you can apply it in any area you want to work on.

A minimum baseline is the minimum amount you expect of yourself. For example, some people have a minimum baseline of flossing once a day. For others, that minimum baseline is once a week. For my children, it's about once every six months at the dentist's office, but we don't need to get into that. I remember once after I had one of my babies I was recuperating and watching Oprah. She was talking about the minimum baseline for changing your sheets. She said, "I change my sheets once a week." Then she looked around nervously. "Is that the standard? Is that still what we're all doing?" She was suddenly unsure if her minimum baseline was socially acceptable.

We all have minimum baselines for almost everything we do. Desiree Linden has a minimum baseline of running 90 miles a week. My minimum baseline for running is about a tenth of that. We have minimum baselines for how often we call or see our parents, or have a night out without the kids, or take a shower, or check our budget, or empty the garbage, or hold team huddles. This is how we accomplish and prioritize the many to-do's in our lives. If there is something we aren't doing, it's because we have not established a minimum baseline for it.

For example, let's say you have a goal to connect with your teenager. You want to show up in the relationship and do what it takes to be more accessible. I recommend that when you set your minimum baseline, you start small. So perhaps your minimum baseline is to eat dinner with them three days a week, with no phones and lots of eye contact. This is the minimum you will do to show up. Week after week as you keep that commitment, not only will your connection increase (achieve your goal) you will honor your word to yourself and become a person who connects with their children regularly.

If you have a goal to eat better, you can set a minimum baseline like eating one vegetable with every dinner or only eating out twice a week. If you have a goal to write a book, establish a minimum baseline of writing for 30 minutes, three days a week. You can increase from there as you keep that commitment with yourself. If you want to make more sales, set a minimum baseline for the number of calls per day. Whatever you want to start, establish your minimum effort and work up from there.

Remember to start small and then keep every seemingly insignificant commitment you make with yourself. You can always increase your minimums, but what is really happening over time is that you are proving to yourself that you are person who keeps their word, shows up, and reaches their goals every time. This is where the principle of showing up gets its power. Keep in mind, that if you find that you cannot meet your minimum baseline, you have simply set it too high. Reduce the minimum and try again.

YOU ARE WHAT YOU DO

Finally, as you begin working at your minimum baseline, you can adjust, remove, and change any labels your brain offers. For example, let's say you want to show up in your life by getting up earlier. You set a minimum baseline that five days a week you are going to get up 15 minutes earlier. Perhaps before you set this minimum baseline, your brain liked to tell you that you are not a morning person. As you keep your minimum baseline, you are proving that you are indeed a morning person. You are what you do. Even if you only do it for a little bit, a few times a week, in that moment you are that person. And the more you do it, the more you become exactly that.

A few years ago, I started lifting weights. I was completely intimidated by "that side of the gym" with all the clanging equipment and grunting men and foreign exercise machines. I was unsure about how to rack the bars or how to operate the various weight machines or even proper form. I was way out of my depth. My brain kept telling me, "You are a runner. You are not a weight lifter. You do not belong here." It kept begging me to go back to my solitary trails in the desert. But I wanted to get faster and I knew I needed more strength to do that, so I persisted.

I set a minimum baseline and put myself on that side of the gym three days a week. Last year, I happened to be at the gym with my husband. As we were leaving, he offhandedly said, "You look just like them. You totally fit in there." Over time, I had become a weight lifter. I had become one by doing what one does.

It is the same for you. Whatever you want to be, you simply need to do—over and over and over again. Set a minimum baseline and then show up. Again and again and again. Every time you do, you become exactly what you are striving to be.

Showing up in any area of your life the way you want to is absolutely possible. From a distance, it looks like magic or a happy accident, but it's always a conscious choice. When you can let go of the need for results and fully commit to doing the work required even when things are hard or painful—when you learn to honor every commitment you make to yourself—there is nothing you can't become.

EXERCISES FOR SHOWING UP

1. Take a look at your life with a curious eye. Where do you notice you are not showing up the way you want to? Where are you living without real commitment?

2. When you look at this area, what is the thought you believe about yourself that is holding you back?

   For example, if you aren't showing up in your job, what do you believe about yourself that prevents you from taking action? Perhaps: "I'm not a go-getter," or "I'm not driven," or "I'm just here for the paycheck."

   Remember, if you aren't taking the action you want, in any area of your life, it's because of a thought you have about yourself. If you aren't taking care of your body the way you want to, perhaps you have a thought like, "I've never been an athlete," or "I don't have willpower," or "I hate exercise."

   Really explore the label that is keeping you from taking action and showing up committed in this area of your life.

3. Once you identify the label holding you back, establish a minimum baseline for the action you will take in this area. The minimum baseline should be small enough to be easily accomplished.

4. Commit to meeting your minimum baseline for one week. (If you can't meet the minimum baseline you will need to reduce the minimum and try again.)

5. As you meet your minimum baseline, recognize and acknowledge that you are a person that is the very opposite of your label.

For example, if you label yourself as a person who doesn't like exercise and you set a minimum baseline to put your shoes on and drive to the gym three days a week, every time you drive to the gym you are a person who exercises. Every time you meet your minimum baseline you reinforce your new identity.

6. Over time you can increase your commitment by increasing your minimum baseline.

For example, you can move from driving to the gym to getting on the treadmill for 10 minutes three days a week. And then five days a week. And then 10 minutes of weights and 10 minutes on the treadmill. You can always do more when you want, but meeting your minimum baseline gives you the confidence that you are a person who knows how to show up in their life. You will be surprised to see this confidence seep into other areas of your life.

After two years in the master's program at Grand Canyon University and 15 years after he started, Magno Santos became a licensed nurse practitioner. He opened his own practice and began caring for patients as he always wanted to. When Magno Santos looks back to see all that he has been able to accomplish, even he is amazed.

"When my father died, I thought if I had known CPR, I could have saved him. This gave me a great desire to be able to help people, but I had no education. Whatever I wanted to do, was not possible because of my lack of education." Magno had dreams but no way to picture his own possibility of accomplishing them. He had no reference for what he could become. He felt unqualified and he also felt powerless to change that.

All that changed when his coworker told him that he was going to school one class at a time. Magno was stunned. The world changed in an instant. He said, "I felt this kind of spark—a great desire inside."

Magno looked at the young man and thought what he always thought, "If he can do it, I can do it." This young man's effort to improve his own life impacted Magno. Before that moment, Magno had no idea what was possible.

The spark was so great, Magno went straight to the community college to enroll, but did not pass the entrance exam. Magno's doubts surfaced and he started to question his ability to do it.

A few days later, his second daughter was born. During labor, Magno got talking to the nurse that was helping his wife. He found out she worked at the hospital full-time and was going to school to become a nurse-midwife. Magno was surprised. He asked her if she had any children. She said, "I have five." Magno couldn't believe it.

"I thought, 'You have five kids and you're working full time and you're going to school. Holy! If you can do it, I can do it. I don't have five kids. I don't work like you do with crazy hours.' And then Amanda was born. I was supposed to be filming her, but I missed it because I was thinking about everything the nurse told me."

The grit and persistence and desire for growth that this delivery nurse displayed again had an impact on Magno. He said, "When we went home, I told my wife, 'I have to go to school.'" That was the beginning.

Other people were growing and pushing themselves towards lofty goals for what it would do for them in their own lives, but it had a ripple effect on Magno. Even the pizza restaurant owner from Pakistan, who came to America and built a small business to improve his own life and the life of his family, inadvertently impacted and lifted Magno.

When we set aside our fears and the many reasons we can't do something or are unqualified to do it, we progress personally, but simultaneously we lift others and allow them to rise with us. Our unqualified success always has a ripple effect.

Magno is now producing his own ripple effect. His story allows others to see what's possible in their own lives. If I can do it, you can do it.

But to do any of it, Magno first had to ignore his inadequacies and shortcomings long enough to try. He said he realized it was bigger than him. "I am coming from a third-world country. I know people who could do better than me. They're much smarter than I am. They could do much more than I can do. But I've been given this opportunity—and I cannot waste it.

"On behalf of myself, on behalf of my children, on behalf of my fellow Brazilians, dreaming of one day coming to America, I have to be successful. I've got to be successful. I cannot not do it."

Magno Santos understands the ripple effect. He knows that in creating his own success, he unintentionally wrote a story of what's possible—for anyone.

CHAPTER 13

RIPPLE EFFECT

---

*"Listen to the mustn'ts, child. Listen to the don'ts.
Listen to the shouldn'ts, the impossibles, the won'ts.
Listen to the never haves, then listen close to me...
Anything can happen, child. Anything can be."*

—Shel Silverstein

In *The Little Book of Talent,* Daniel Coyle examined the phenomenon of hotbeds of talent—places and periods of time where clusters of great talent appeared simultaneously. He looked at several pockets of modern achievement in sports, academics, and the arts, to discover what exactly was happening to create a burst of great players or artists or geniuses where none had been before.

He studied these hotbeds—places like the Spartak Tennis Club in Moscow and the Septien School of Contemporary Music in Dallas, the North Baltimore Aquatic Club, KIPP charter schools, and Meadowmount School of Music, just to name a few—wondering what they all had in common and taking notes about what he found.

CLUSTERS OF GREATNESS

What Coyle was observing, of course, was not a new phenomenon. Throughout history, there have been moments in time and space where clusters of greatness, or "talent clots," as David Banks called them, have appeared.

Think of the explosion in thought and philosophy that occurred in Athens over a period of 60 years in the 4th century BC. After thousands of years of human history, in this one place bloomed a cluster of geniuses that basically invented the principles of Western civilization, including Plato, Socrates, Thucydides, Euripides, Aeschylus, Herodotus, and Aristophanes.

Florence, Italy in the last half of the 15th century saw a similar talent cluster, with a staggering number of brilliant artists like Michelangelo, Ghiberti, Botticelli, Donatello, and da Vinci, reinventing the way we experienced art and creating a new vision of what was possible with paint and stone and other mediums.

Writers Hemingway, Fitzgerald, Eliot, Joyce, Miller, Pound and Stein all lived and worked in Paris in the 1920s. While in the 60s, the Detroit music scene produced Diana Ross & The Supremes, Stevie Wonder, Marvin Gaye, The Jackson 5, Gladys Knight & the Pips, among many others.

It is no different in business than it is in the arts. William Hewlett, David Packard, Robert Helliwell, Edward Ginzton, O.G. Villard Jr., and William B. Shockley, all came out of Stanford in the 1930s studying with Frederick Terman, the acknowledged father of Silicon Valley.

So, what is happening when these clusters of greatness arise? Is it the random workings of a mischievous universe, or the astounding appearance of meta-ideas concentrated in a single area, or some strange permutation of the law of attraction? Perhaps it's just the perfect environment for growth or the exact right combination of healthy competition? What creates talent in such concentrated and obvious clusters?

The primary factor, I believe, was best explained in a recent interview with NFL safety, actor, and playwright, Bo Eason.

IF HE'S GOING, I'M GOING

Bo Eason, a former NFL safety, said that when he read Coyle's book, he realized that he had been a part of these hotbeds of talent nearly everywhere he had gone throughout his life.

When Eason was in high school, he played on the football team with 26 other farm boys. The high school Bo attended had never produced an NFL player in its history, nor has one come out of the school since Bo graduated. But when Bo Eason was there, out of 27 players on that one team, four of them went on to play in the NFL.

To give you some context, out of the 1.2 million high school football players, 0.08% go on to play in the NFL. But in this one high school, at this particular period in time, the odds were one out of six. As Bo says, "That's a statistical impossibility. It can't happen."

But it did.

Eason points out he was one of the smallest on the team and as he characterizes it, "not that good," but Eason had a dream. He wanted to play in the NFL and he wanted to be the best safety in the world. He made a plan when he was nine years old and nothing was going to stop him.

Years later, Bo asked the other three NFL players why it happened the way it did, how the four of them all ended up in the NFL. They told him it was because he was always carrying his plan around and telling people he was going to be the best safety in the world. And they thought, "If that little guy Bo's doing it, I'm doing it too."

As Eason tells it, "It's just that one guy, the smallest guy, and not that good, had a dream. And kept saying, 'I'm going to go do this dream' and these guys said, 'Well, I'll just go too then. If he's going, I'm going.'"[27]

Eason concluded, "Every time I've made a plan and followed it, other people come with me."

AN EXAMPLE OF WHAT'S POSSIBLE

It turns out that what Eason describes is not unreasonable or impossible. Studies have proven that even small, insignificant exposure to a role model has the power to greatly increase unconscious motivation. For example, in one study, students were told that they shared a birthday with a mathematician—they didn't know the mathematician nor had they ever actually even heard of them. They were simply told they shared a birthday with them.

The students were then asked to solve a set of difficult math problems. Remarkably, these students put in 62% more effort in trying to solve the math tasks than the control group who was not given the birthday information.

Before 1997 there were no South Korean golfers on the Ladies Professional Golf Association (LPGA) Tour. But today there are more than 40 and they win more than a third of all the tournaments played. What was the cause of such a massive shift in achievement? One golfer, Se Ri Pak, won two major tournaments in 1998. This one woman changed the expectation and the possibilities for hundreds of South Korean girls by giving them a new vision of what was possible. South Korean

---

[27] "Face The ODDS - Bo Eason | Inside Quest #36." Video file, 42:08. YouTube. Posted by Tom Bilyeu Classics, May 14, 2017. Accessed November 12, 2018. https://www.youtube.com/watch?v=ptnT1DwuN0o.

golfer, Christina Kim, explained this idea perfectly, "If she can do it, why can't I?"

What Eason and Pak were able to do is to create a new vision of what's possible. Once they proved it could be done, others could believe it too. When it's done right, as we set our sights on bigger goals and higher expectations for ourselves, we can lift those around us at the same time.

BIG PICTURE

Mariam Naficy is the founder and CEO of Minted, which started as an online stationery retailer. She had an idea to create a stationery company using a crowdsourcing model to offer customized card designs. The company started with save-the-date cards for weddings. Surprisingly, lots of their customers chose designs that included a photo. Naficy said, "I remember a national printer saying to me, 'Mariam, in our business, people do not put photos on their save-the-date cards.' I thought to myself, 'That's funny, because consumers seem to be voting for them.'"[28] Mariam's firm belief in her original crowdsourcing idea, her confidence in the talent of her artists, and her certainty that her customers knew what they wanted, changed the entire market. Today, almost 100 percent of save-the-date cards have a photo on them.

Even more importantly, Minted not only offered their customers a completely different product in the marketplace, they created a whole new platform for artists, designers, and creatives all over the world. Naficy recalls, "It wasn't long before there was a whole community of designers on the site, and illustrators and artists. And their work was selling."

---

[28] Lagorio-Chafkin, Christine, ed. "This Founder Almost Shut Down Her Design Business After Year 1. Now It Has 400 Employees and a 9-Figure Revenue." Inc. Last modified February 26, 2019. Accessed February 26, 2019. https://www.inc.com/christine-lagorio/minted-mariam-naficy-founders-project.html.

Naficy and her investors soon realized that their "stationery model" had even bigger potential to offer art prints, wall murals, and even textiles. Minted began to broaden its offerings and got some industry pushback. Mariam said, "A lot of the establishment people we would talk to would ask: 'Well, who are these artists anyway?' I would get that question over and over again from people who could not accept the fact that there were people who could not afford to go to design school or art school, and yet could teach themselves and in a blind competition actually win."

Mariam Naficy built her little idea into a $100M business and created a ripple effect, giving opportunities to 15,000-plus people who had never had the chance to produce and sell their art. "Many of these artists and designers are transitioning from other careers like, for example, an Alaskan oil rig worker and a master plumber in New York. I would say probably 20 percent of the designers probably are fully making a living from Minted."

We never work in a vacuum. As we grow and build our own dreams, the beautiful thing is that we help others build theirs as well.

MAGIC CARPET RIDE

Russ Palmer, who has been instrumental in my personal and professional growth, is the perfect example of this kind of leadership—the kind that creates a ripple effect of growth around them.

When Russ started out, he was a college student, using an old van to do carpet cleaning in order to pay his way through school. At that point, he had no experience running a company, managing employees, or operating a major enterprise. It wasn't even in his line of sight.

Russ started small. He didn't know much about restoration services or drying techniques, but he was fascinated by the science behind it. He started to learn more, at the beginning, mostly out of pure curiosity. But the more he learned, the more he saw the potential for his own growth. "I started to see I could really do something with this," he said. Without really knowing how, he started a bare-bones restoration company that was solely focused on water damage.

It was a good little company that did excellent work. Russ learned everything he could about the industry and worked hard to improve the methods he used on his losses. And it paid off. He became known as one of the leading water damage experts in the area with other professionals seeking him out for knowledge and opinions. It wasn't long before he was dragging his little brothers around with him on losses sharing his knowledge with them. They soon became his first employees and several of them are still in the industry, making a name for themselves. (Ripple effect.)

The more experience Russ got, the bigger his dreams got. He wanted to be the best restoration company in Phoenix. There were lots of big industry players already well-established, but Russ knew that a superior restoration product would give him the edge. As Russ's technical abilities grew so did the company's bottom line. Russ used the growth to expand the team's knowledge, training, and service lines. The company started restoring losses from fires and mold in addition to water damage, and the little company was making a reliable $1-$2M every year.

Russ could see that the bigger he grew his business, the more people he could employ. This was his ultimate dream—to be able to impact the lives and families of the people around him. How many people could he employ? How great could he make their work environment by having the best company culture? How could he impact an individual's growth and development? Russ decided to raise the stakes. He challenged his team to set bigger goals and expand their vision. This would mean bigger clients, bigger jobs, and bigger risk.

In order to make the leap from $1M to $7M to $22M, things had to change often. We had to change our processes, increase our accountability, require more from ourselves, and revisit our strategy over and over. None of it was easy. In seeking to grow his business, Russ was growing all of us in the process.

The company made a concerted push into commercial markets and healthcare restoration. It opened an environmental services division to handle hazardous materials and went through the certification and training required to do it. At every stage the company hired, trained, and employed more people. The ripples kept coming.

Russ's whole mission and aim for owning his company is to provide a way for others to create an amazing life for themselves and their families. In fact, his big, hairy, audacious goal is to create a business that supports 125 families who are net promoters. The motivation behind this is solely about giving others an avenue to success and not about what it will do for him as a business owner. He wants to grow the capacity and potential of his team more than he wants to grow his brand or his bottom line or his ego. Russ Palmer has figured out the ripple effect and it is pushing him to continually expand the boundaries of his success. He's going places, and he's bringing his team with him.

THE SCARCITY LIE

The inclination to build and invest in others as you progress in your own journey is not a natural one. Contrary to Russ Palmer's philosophy, most of us spend our lives trying to earn the credit, take the credit, and get the credit. There is a deep, primal fear that there is never enough to go around, and that there is an inherent scarcity of resources and recognition in the world.

As research scientist Brené Brown points out, we let scarcity and fear drive our actions. "We wake up in the morning and we say, 'I didn't get enough sleep.' And we hit the pillow saying, 'I didn't get enough done.' We're never thin enough, extraordinary enough or good enough—until we decide that we are. For me, the opposite of scarcity is not abundance. It's *enough*. I'm enough. My kids are enough."

We have to fight against our primitive brain that points out, with alarm, that there is currently only one mammoth to eat and we have no way of knowing when we'll get another one. Don't share. If someone else gets some, you get less. That's the law of nature. However, this fear, like the others we have talked about is baseless, archaic, and will not serve you. Not only is there more mammoth where that one came from, there is a world of abundance available. The reality is that the pie is infinite!

There is enough for anyone who wants some. There is enough personal development, achievement, money, recognition, learning, advancement, and improvement for anyone that wants it. Even better, the more you give and the more you build, the more you will get in return. Figuring that out sooner rather than later will change everything as you climb your way from unqualified to success.

APPARENTLY, ANYTHING IS POSSIBLE

In many ways the unqualified among us are best positioned to help others rise as we pursue and achieve our goals and do our work in the world. This is because, like those who went with Bo Eason to the NFL and those who followed Se Ri Pak to winning golf tournaments, there was a general feeling that neither Eason or Pak were anything special—that if they could make it, then surely others could as well.

When Roger Banister beat the world record for the 4-minute mile, he was not the fastest runner in the world. In fact, there were many in his field who felt they were superior runners. Mere weeks after Banister beat the record, other runners went on to reset the record with even faster times. Other runners just needed to know it was possible. And when it was accomplished by someone who was not a prodigy or a phenomenon, even better.

Using your averageness and admitted inadequacies while still working to achieve greatness in your field, gives others around you a vision for what is possible for them as well. In fact, that very authenticity can make all the difference for those around you as they work to accomplish hard things.

There is a story told about a mother who brought her son to visit Gandhi to receive instruction and wisdom because he was eating too much sugar. Gandhi was the boy's idol. The mother believed that if Gandhi told the boy to stop then he would.

Instead, Gandhi told the mother and son to come back in two weeks.

Two weeks later, the pair returned and Gandhi looked directly at the boy and told him to stop eating sugar. The boy promised to change and improve his behavior.

The mother, perplexed and frustrated, asked why she had to wait for two weeks for Gandhi to talk to her son about his sugar consumption. Gandhi simply replied, "Two weeks ago I was just like your boy, eating too much sugar."

Gandhi could not ask the boy to rise to a higher standard than he himself was living.

As you work to overcome fears, move through failure, work with grit and persistence, continually and humbly learn and grow, others will come with you. Your own quest for improvement and growth, in spite of your insecurities and shortcomings, gives others the courage to follow. All that is required is to do your best to work and evolve and become a higher version of yourself. As you do so, others will find hope and motivation to continue their own work.

NOT THROWING AWAY MY SHOT

By any standard, Lin-Manuel Miranda's musical, *Hamilton,* is one of the greatest ever written. But in the beginning, it seemed like an insane concept and an impossible endeavor. Miranda had an idea to write a big Broadway musical about an 18th century Treasury Secretary. (There might not be a more "unqualified" idea ever.)

As crazy as it was, Miranda believed whole-heartedly in his unlikely idea and started writing. As he wrote, he could picture the characters as his personal rap heroes—Jay Z, Lil Wayne, Common, Busta Rhymes. He decided that not only would he write a musical about a Treasury Secretary, but it would be done in rap. Again, the whole idea looked like a recipe for disaster. It was hard to say how any of this would be received by an audience used to the traditional musical ballad.

Miranda went to work transforming the ancient, dusty words of the past into riveting rap battles, and turning one-dimensional archetypes from American history into real people. Bay area rapper, Daveed Diggs told Rolling Stone, "When you're developing your voice as a rapper, you figure out your cadence—your swag—and that's how you write. Lin managed to figure that out for *all* of these different characters—everyone has their own swag, and it feels germane to them. And that's really impressive."[29]

[29] Binelli, Mark. "'Hamilton' Mania! Backstage at the Cultural Event of Our Time." *Rolling Stone*, June 1, 2016. https://www.rollingstone.com/culture/culture-news/

Once Miranda could see the characters coming to life through the raps, he took it one step further. Though the play was about the Founding Fathers, a decidedly white, mostly-privileged group of men, Miranda envisioned their roles being played by a multi-racial cast that represented the current diversity of the country.

When he went to cast the show his message was, "I know this is about the Founding Fathers, but there's work for you here!" The show's enthusiastic reception and its unqualified success forever changed the way Broadway sees all of its actors and performers and opened new possibilities for every actor performing in every show after that. Additionally, it allowed the audience—whoever they were—to see themselves in the story.

"It is quite literally taking the history that someone has tried to exclude us from and reclaiming it," says Leslie Odom Jr., who almost stole the show playing Aaron Burr. "We are saying we have the right to tell it too."

All this because Lin-Manuel Miranda had a (probably bad) idea and didn't let the (justifiable) parade of doubts dissuade him from his goal. The power of the ripple effect is that it gives others a different vision of what's possible. Miranda was pursuing his own goals, his own evolution, his own dreams, and he lifted an entire industry and its audiences with him.

THE POWER OF ONE

In 2014, Naval Admiral William H. McRaven delivered the commencement address for the University of Texas at Austin. In the speech, McRaven talked about the lessons he learned in the grueling days of Navy SEAL training.

---

hamilton-mania-backstage-at-the-cultural-event-of-our-time-44203/.

He relayed that the ninth week of SEAL training is referred to as "Hell Week." This week is a brutal test of physical and mental strength, with six days of no sleep, constant physical and mental harassment, and one horrific day spent at the Mud Flats. The Mud Flats are an area between Tijuana, Mexico and San Diego, CA, where the water runs off and creates the Tijuana Slough—a huge, swampy, salt marsh, where the mud can swallow you whole.

McRaven described how one day they paddled down to the mud flats, and as the sun began to set his training class was ordered into the mud. The mud was freezing cold and the wind was howling. The mud consumed each man until there was nothing showing but their heads sticking out of the swampy sludge.

The SEAL instructors told them that they could leave the mud if only five of the men quit. "If just five men gave up," McRaven recounted, "we could get out of the oppressive cold. Looking around the mud flat it was apparent that some students were about to give up. It was still over eight hours till the sun came up—eight more hours of bone chilling cold."[30]

McRaven said that over the chattering teeth and the shivering, desperate moans of the trainees in his class, one voice began to sing and echo across the mud, terribly out of tune, but strong and enthusiastic.

McRaven recalled, "One voice became two and two became three and before long everyone in the class was singing. We knew that if one man could rise above the misery then others could as well."

---

[30] *UT News* (Austin, TX). "Adm. McRaven Urges Graduates to Find Courage to Change the World." May 16, 2014. https://news.utexas.edu/2014/05/16/mcraven-urges-graduates-to-find-courage-to-change-the-world/.

We have cited countless examples of the impact that one person's confidence and certainty can have on others around them to allow them to rise and accomplish impossible things. McRaven's story confirms that even the toughest of us sometimes need the perspective of someone else, believing the impossible, to motivate and help us move forward in our darkest hours. Each of us will have moments to be exactly that for someone else when it counts the most.

THE POWER OF MANY

Just as we have the power to lift and build those around us, the magic of this kind of thinking and this way of living is that it offers those of us who feel unqualified an incredibly powerful gift in return.

Bo Eason admits that most nights he doesn't want to go out on stage and perform his one-man, self-written play. Backstage, his mind tempts him with the idea of running for the stage door, getting in a cab, and never coming back.

He says it was no different for him in the NFL, waiting in the tunnel to go out onto the field, when the nerves and the fear and the anxiety were impossibly heavy to bear. Eason talks about these moments in his life when he is surrounded by cinderblocks on every side—under stadiums, in long tunnels leading to well-lit fields, and backstage in hundreds of dark theatres. And as he stands there surrounded by cinderblocks, there is a cinderblock of fear and dread sitting in his chest as well.

"It's your turn," he says. "There's so much isolation and loneliness in that moment, where only you have to decide if you're going or not."

In those moments, when the impulse to run and hide is so high, when the temptation to be invisible and live an invisible life where no one can judge you is pulling and clawing at you to quit, Bo Eason says:

> *"I think of the audience. I think of my teammates. And I think If I don't go out, we could lose. If I don't go out, we will probably lose. It becomes bigger than me. I'm the performer, but then I think of the other people who I'm going to let down if I don't take that step forward. That's what football taught me the most. You're going to have to come through for your team at the toughest moment."*

For Bo Eason, other people are the leverage point.

Remember that all of this brave work among the cinderblocks is optional. He could have chosen an easier, quieter, safer path. But he chose the way of challenge and growth. He expected more of himself. And in those moments when his fear is overwhelming, when he feels inadequate and unqualified and utterly lacking, he remembers that people are counting on him. Yes, his life's work has lifted others. But in those moments of decision, at the moment of great alarm, they lift him as well. Their dependence and need allow him to do the hardest things he has to do.

That is the gift of doing your work for the sake of others, even inadvertently. It becomes bigger than you. For the Navy SEALS, for Bo Eason, for Mariam Naficy, and Si Re Pak, Russ Palmer, and countless unqualified others, this is the secret pool of power and motivation when things get hard. As you work towards your own goals and see the ripple effect it has on others, it will give you the leverage to do the impossible, over and over again.

EXERCISES TO CREATE THE RIPPLE EFFECT

1. Share knowledge freely. Using your blog or email list, regularly offer your subscribers useful, free information to help them build their businesses or improve their lives.

2. Create a skills matrix for your team. Identify two areas of growth for each individual and collaborate with them on a development plan where they can work and develop these skills.

3. Find one person in your extended network that you can invest in their growth and development. Choose someone whose success won't benefit you in any way. As you invest in their success and growth, notice the positive impact it has upon you and your own growth.

4. Focus only on the accomplishments of others. Spend one week avoiding taking credit for anything, but instead noticing and pointing out the contributions of everyone around you.

5. Adopt a zero-gossip policy. Give people the benefit of the doubt. Readily admit that you don't have all the information and refuse to share anything that does not build and promote others.

6. Our brains automatically notice the negative. They were designed to be on the lookout for problems or trouble. For an hour, every time your brain notices a problem or offers a negative thought, replace it with a positive one.

    For example, I have to take my daughter to school at 6:30 am so she can attend a religious seminary class as part of her school day. This means if I want to get to the gym before I start my day, I have to get up at 4:30. Whenever I have the thought that it's ridiculous that we have to get up so early, I replace it with a thought like, "I'm grateful she's committed enough to get up and go so early." Or "I'm grateful we get a chance to sacrifice for what's important to us." Or even, "I'm grateful I have a car that gets us where we need to be."

After mastering one hour, try increasing to two hours, half a day, a whole day. Get in the habit of recognizing the positive.

CHAPTER 14

UNQUALIFIED <u>AND</u> SUCCESSFUL

"If you're waiting for permission you'll be waiting forever."
—*Adam Smiley Poswolsky*

In early 2018, Dennis Deaton, a successful author and corporate educator, had a cough that wouldn't go away. Occasionally it was accompanied by slight queasiness, but overall, he felt good and healthy, recently completing a 400-mile bike ride across part of Maine.

Dennis had a bout of Valley Fever in 2014 and he kind of shrugged off the symptomatic cough, thinking that he might just be having a reoccurrence of that old illness.

This story might have had a very different ending, but Magno Santos just happened to be his neighbor. One day, Dennis had the thought that he should just call Magno and see if he could come by the hospital and get a quick chest x-ray to rule out Valley Fever.

When he called, Magno was at home. He explained his symptoms and said he'd like to come by for an x-ray sometime. Instead of agreeing, Magno said, "I'll be right there."

Five minutes later, Magno was at his front door, with his roller bag in hand. He had shown up at Dennis's house with his little mobile clinic, as it were, ready to do an assessment. He performed a thorough exam, listening to Dennis's chest, taking vitals, and carefully making notes. Then he told his patient that he thought he had some situational brachycardia going on and that his heart was beating too slowly. Magno asked him if he felt dizzy or lightheaded.

Magno recommended that he go see a cardiologist. He said he knew a good one and immediately called and got him in, setting up the appointment for two days later.

The next day, Magno called Dennis and recommended that he get a blood test before he went to the cardiologist. He explained that this was just good standard of care. He wanted the specialist to have as much data and information as possible at the appointment.

Magno ordered the blood test and got the results later that day.

He called Dennis after getting the results and asked, "Do you have a fever? Or any place on your body that's sore or red?"

"No."

Magno said, "Well, something is going on. Your white count's way too high."

Dennis again said he couldn't think of any reason why that would be. Magno told him, "I'm going to prescribe an antibiotic. After the cardiologist makes his assessment, we may need to do more tests, but we can start by addressing this possible infection."

The next day, the cardiologist looked at the lab results and offhandedly asked Dennis how he was managing his blood disease.

Dennis said he didn't have a blood disease.

The cardiologist said, "Yes you do. You have leukemia. You didn't know that?"

That was the day my dad found out he had cancer.

If Magno hadn't been there and taken the action he had—showing up at my parents' house, ordering the blood tests, recommending the cardiologist, setting up an immediate appointment—my dad's illness would not have been diagnosed for many months while the leukemia replicated unchecked in his bloodstream. Magno's persistence, high standard of care, and dedication to his work made an enormous difference in my dad's treatment protocol and prognosis. In many ways, my dad owes his life to Magno's meticulous care.

For an unqualified young man who dared to dream of one day delivering pizzas, Magno Santos certainly exceeded even his own expectations.

As I think about Magno's unlikely story, all the ups and downs, the point where he started, the places he could have stopped, and the destination where he ended up, I am humbled to realize that my own life would be dramatically different if Magno was a different kind of person—if he was the kind of person that accepted his limitations as fact, or the kind of person that accepted that being unqualified was simply the way things would always be.

Because Magno refused to accept that his *reality*—at any point in his journey—was his *final destiny,* he earned the ability to make an impact on the lives of countless people, my life and my family's life among them.

As Henry James said, "We work in the dark—we do what we can—we give what we have." Or we don't. We are either brave and belligerent in the face of our inadequacies, or we're not. We either ignore and inoculate our self-doubts, or we don't. Magno always had a choice. And there are more than a few people in this world that are glad he made the ones he did.

NOTHING SPECIAL

Too many of us believe that the feelings of being unqualified or inadequate don't apply to people who achieve. We think that people who reach their goals are fundamentally different because they not only *became* qualified, somehow, they *started* qualified.

When you look at Magno's story, you can clearly see this is not the case. When he started, there was not a more unqualified position to be in. I have related his story so that you can see that it's not people with extraordinary ability, extraordinary luck, or extraordinary advantages that achieve what they want. It's only people with the extraordinary ability to see their own "un-qualification" and *not let it matter at all.*

Magno knew he was unqualified, just as you may. Magno had lots to learn to become who and what he wanted to be, just as you do. But what made Magno's story different is that he believed that he didn't have to be extraordinary in order to accomplish what he wanted. He saw the truth—regular, everyday people were doing what he wanted to do. And he knew if they could do it, so could he.

No matter what you want to do, regular people are doing it. When we look at others and see them as extraordinary, we dismiss our own ability to do what they are doing. As I once heard Lisa Nichols say, "You want to make me extraordinary to let yourself off the hook."

MORE THAN ORDINARY

My dad is one of the most talented and gifted corporate educators in the world. He has spent his life teaching people in Fortune 500 companies a lot of the same principles we have discussed in this book. His seminars on Ownership Spirit, and Destination Thinking for Leaders have been transformational to thousands. After he read the first draft of this book, he told me a story from one of his seminars.

Imagine a room full of people, enraptured and engaged as my dad teaches the principles of growth and achievement, highlighting examples of well-known figures who have overcome incredible odds to become the successes they are. People are moved and inspired.

And then in the back of the room, a hand is raised. A woman stands up and says, "You have just spent the last several hours telling us the stories of famous, incredible, talented people. Look around here. We are just ordinary people."

My dad stood there as silence permeated the room. And just when you might think the whole seminar took a turn for the worse, he said, "You are right. These people are extraordinary!"

And then he paused, searching for a way to counter the implied short-sell of herself and everyone else in the room, to discredit the fallacy that successful people are innately superior to the rest of us common folks. Then the words came to him and he said, "You have just pinpointed the most important truth you can ever realize: Extraordinary people are ordinary people that discover that *ordinary people* have *extraordinary capabilities*." The seminar just skyrocketed from there, and it was one of the most successful of his career.

Nobody starts out extraordinary. No one begins fully qualified and ready. The minute we understand this principle and it really sinks in, our whole world opens up.

THE UNIVERSAL CONDITION

The goal of this book has not been to magically make you feel qualified. To do that would require a fundamental restructuring of the human brain, which naturally identifies our weak spots and the potential threats to our identity and safety as part of its proper function.

Among those with normal functioning brains and the doubts that come with them are achievers like Nobel Laureate Maya Angelou who said, "I have written eleven books, but each time I think, 'Uh oh, they're going to find out now. I've run a game on everybody, and they're going to find me out'" and Kate Winslet, who admitted, "I wake up in the morning before going off to a shoot, and I think, I can't do this; I'm a fraud."

Do you see? Feeling unqualified is the rule, not the exception. From artists to business leaders, from those in finance to the fine arts, this is the one thing we all have in common. You're in good company. As Jim Gaffigan joked, "Most of the time, I feel entirely unqualified to be a parent. I call these times being awake."

Here's the bad news: If you are waiting for the feeling of qualification—the permission slip, the stamp of approval, or the seal of authenticity—you may wait forever. We think we need society, or the industry we're in, or our families, or our degrees to tell us that we are qualified. Do you remember when Sally Field won the Oscar? After years in the industry, she exclaimed in surprise from the stage, "You like me! You really like me!"

And now the good news: It doesn't matter. You don't have to feel qualified to do any of it. Every achiever felt unqualified and achieved anyway. Remarkably, success is not dependent on *feeling* qualified. We've had it wrong. Success is only dependent on if, in the face of those universal feelings, we do our work in the world anyway.

The tools we have talked about throughout this book are meant to empower you as an ordinary, unqualified person to manage your mind and accomplish your goals even when you're scared, even when you want to quit, even when you fail, even when it's hard, even when it seems your own brain is working against you.

THE UNIVERSAL CHOICE

What about you?

Given the universal condition—that you're never going to be more *first*, that you're never going to know *enough* to do it right the first time, that you're never going to evolve *sufficiently* to achieve a satisfactory feeling of qualification—what are you going to choose?

Are you going to be an ordinary person who does extraordinary things by managing your mind, believing hard, and exercising your deep grit and persistence? Are you going to ignore your fears, embrace your vulnerability, and learn from your failures? Will you show up, so hungry for growth and a willingness to begin where you are, that your steady progress toward your vision of what's possible brings others with you?

You always get to choose. Success won't just happen. For any of us.

I know from where you stand it might look impossible and improbable and unbelievable.

But choose to believe it anyway.

I know other people and your very own brain will tell you it's too hard, it's takes too long, or it's just crazy.

Choose to do it anyway.

I know some people think it doesn't matter, that ordinary is fine, that there's something to be said for contentment and ease.

Choose to tell yourself the truth.

It's all there for anyone that wants it. What is it you want?

Will you pay attention to the salt wounds and the height of the cliff, to the voices that say you can't build a business around chicken salad or dream about being a safety in the NFL? Will you listen to the statistics of people who stay sober, to the newspapers who say you're done, or the terrified thoughts that say you'll never operate on another heart again. Will you surrender to the fires that burn your dreams to the ground, or the relentless barrage of evidence that you have no business doing what you're doing, or the fact that you don't know a single word of English?

Will you spend your time and your energy noticing all of these obstacles and "realities," or will you simply accept them as part of the process, the price of admission, and then get busy achieving your dreams anyway?

Remember, you always get to choose.

Come join the rest of the unqualified, ordinary, regular human beings who want more and know that more is possible for everyone that is willing to do the work—the constant, internal, mental work—that is the fee for every dream you've ever had.

Imagine what an army of unqualified, action-driven, results-committed people can do in the world. Who will you bring with you? How far can you go? For ordinary people willing to do extraordinary things (believe, grow, persist, fail, show up) with great courage, vulnerability, and vision, there is no limit to what we can achieve.

Choose to be an unqualified success! And choose it again and again, for as long as it takes.

EXERCISES TO BE AN UNQUALIFIED SUCCESS

1. What is your dream?

2. What action would you take if you were perfectly qualified to achieve it?

3. Why are you choosing not to take this action? Tell yourself the truth.

4. What are you willing to require of yourself so that you can achieve your dream?

5. Record your commitment on our website and hold yourself accountable. There is nothing you can't achieve if you choose to.

ABOUT THE AUTHOR

Rachel Stewart started as an unqualified office manager, but over the last decade has worked to become the Executive Vice President of Titan Restoration of Arizona, helping to build operations from $2M to $22M, with a primary focus on accountability, profitability and company culture.

Rachel became the co-founder and CEO of a software development company in 2018, focused on getting contractors the technology tools they need to do their work more efficiently.

Over the years, Rachel learned that the only limitations to her success are in her own mind.

In *Unqualified Success* Rachel Stewart shares the tools that made all the difference in her achievement in a practical and engaging way. The things she learned the hard way are made available in this easily accessible format for anyone who wants to take their life to the next level.

Rachel lives in Mesa, Arizona with her husband and four brilliant children. She volunteers actively in her community. When she's not building her company, improving her industry, or writing books, she is likely to be found on a long run through the desert trails near her home.

Printed in Great Britain
by Amazon